AMERICAN ADOBES

Rural Houses
of Northern New Mexico

AMERICAN ADOBES

Rural Houses of Northern New Mexico

Beverley Spears

University of New Mexico Press
Albuquerque

Library of Congress Cataloging-in-Publication Data

Spears, Beverley, 1945–
   American adobes.

   Bibliography: p.
   Includes index.
   1. Adobe houses—New Mexico. 2. Architecture,
Domestic—New Mexico. 3. Vernacular architecture—
New Mexico. I. Title.
NA7235.N6S64 1986   728'.09789   86-11219
ISBN 0-8263-0889-9
ISBN 0-8263-0896-1 (pbk.)

Design: Barbara Jellow

Library of Congress Cataloging in Publication Data

Contents

for
Julia

Preface

The title of this book, *American Adobes*, is a tribute to the unique status of the New Mexico village adobes within the architecture of the United States. These adobe houses were built by Hispanic Americans who gradually developed a particular architectural style as they modified their Spanish Colonial building traditions to reflect American influences. These are houses built at a time when most Americans were attempting to conform to mainstream national tastes and values rather than to perpetuate ethnic and regional differences. Although the rural villagers had neither the affluence nor the exposure to national architectural styles necessary to duplicate popular American houses of the period, they did select certain motifs, details, and forms which could be incorporated into their local building customs. As more and more American features were adopted, these adobe houses became American in an original way.

The area of the study, which is shown on the map on page x was loosely defined as the central mountain area of northern New Mexico. The boundaries seemed to fall into place easily and without deliberation, with the exception of Wagon Mound. That town has some interesting old owner-built adobe houses, yet they are situated on a regular grid of wide, straight streets developed by speculators when the railroad was built. The striking contrast between Wagon Mound and the villages of central northern New Mexico helps bring into focus the unique quality of the northern villages as compared to the typical little towns of the western United States.

The photographs were all taken between September 1983 and November 1985.

Acknowledgments

The National Endowment for the Arts provided, with what seemed like blind faith, the financial support for the initial study from which this book has grown. Colonel Charles Banks helped me organize and conduct the field-work. I am very grateful to the people of northern New Mexico, who graciously talked to me about their houses and showed them to me. The staff at the New Mexico State Records Center and Archives, Museum of New Mexico History Bureau, State of New Mexico Historic Preservation Division, and the New Mexico State Library were all generous with their expertise. Carole Cristiano skillfully edited the first manuscript. Myra Ellen Jenkins helped me get the historical facts straight. I apologize to her if any transgressions remain. Ellen Harland performed the final proofreading, and Jim Gavin oversaw the correct spelling of all Spanish words and names. My sincerest thanks to all those named and unnamed who have helped me with this project. Final thanks to the staff at UNM Press for the exacting work of transforming a manuscript into a book.

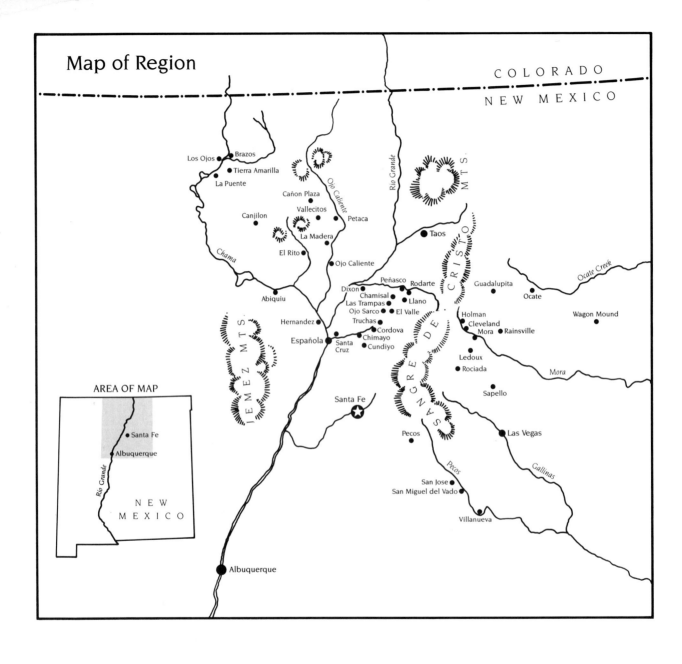

Map of Region

COLORADO
NEW MEXICO

Los Ojos ● ● Brazos
● Tierra Amarilla
La Puente ●

Cañon Plaza
Vallecitos ●
Canjilon ● ● Petaca
La Madera ●
El Rito ●
Ojo Caliente ●

Chama

Rio Grande

Ojo Caliente

● Taos

Ocate Creek

SANGRE DE CRISTO MTS.

Peñasco ● Rodarte
Dixon ● Guadalupita
Chamisal ● Llano ● Ocate
Las Trampas ●
Ojo Sarco ● ● El Valle
Hernandez ● Truchas ● Holman Wagon Mound
● Cordova Cleveland
Española ● Chimayo Mora ● Rainsville
Santa Cruz ● Cundiyo
Ledoux
Rociada
JEMEZ MTS.
Sapello
Santa Fe ☆
Pecos ● Las Vegas
Gallinas

AREA OF MAP

● Santa Fe

● Albuquerque

Rio Grande

NEW MEXICO

Pecos
San Jose ●
San Miguel del Vado ●
Villanueva ●

● Albuquerque

Today

Today in northern New Mexico there are dozens of small villages along the meager rivers and streams flowing out of the Sangre de Cristo Mountains and the high country to the north. These villages are Hispanic in origin, and many have existed for centuries. Often they are rather tight clusters of tin-roofed adobe houses with a church, a few little stores, and probably a gas station. These settlements look different from the average ranching and farming towns in America because they are Spanish Colonial in origin and because the buildings themselves have a distinct appearance and are found nowhere else in the country.

The villages recall an era when small-scale ranching and farming was the way of life and the sole support for many rural communities. The people who inhabit the villages today rely primarily on other sources of income, either salaries from employment in urban areas, pensions and benefits, or income from local jobs which are all too few. Consequently, the villages are waning, and many have an aura of abandoned stillness tempered by signs of ongoing life—occasional cars and pickups on the road, horses in the field, clothes on the line, corn and pumpkins on the portal, and geraniums in the window. Here and there the

1

tall, pale grasses grow high around an abandoned house. The metal gate is fastened tight with baling wire and the path from the gate to the portal is completely grown over. A big black and white magpie sits on a nearby fence post, then swoops down into the grasses across the road. Next to a suburban-looking house and a little way behind a mobile home sits another old house. It used to be a little bigger, but at least one room has been "thrown down," exposing an interior adobe wall with light green paint over mud plaster. The gable roof is so old that the sheets of corrugated metal are rusted deep brown and are warped and curled up along the edges like dry autumn leaves. The house, with its walls of dirt, roof of steel, and its doors and windows of painted wood, has the simplicity and beauty of a handmade tool.

Most of the old houses, whether inhabited or not, are in poor condition, but collectively, along with the dirt roads, the acequias, the old wooden barns and corrals, and the cottonwoods, locust trees, and fruit trees of every sort, they form the fabric of dozens and dozens of little rural villages, each unique in layout and physical setting.

The northern New Mexico villages were established at locations where the river valley was wide and level enough to be irrigated. Ditches or acequias channeled water out of the river upstream and carried it generally parallel to the river. The land between the river and the acequia could be irrigated by opening gates and allowing the water to flow over the land and back toward the river. The Spanish who settled these villages were adept at this method of irrigation, which had been practiced widely in Spain since the time of the Moorish occupation.

In the early days of this region's settlement there was conflict between the Spanish tradition of a dense plaza-oriented town which could be easily controlled and defended, and the single-household structure on the land from which the land could be more easily worked and guarded.[1] The villages today show the influence of each of these forces. Towns such as Córdova, San José, and Chimayó are primarily plaza-oriented while others such as Ojo Sarco and Ojo Caliente are dispersed along the river just above the acequias and the fields. Llano and Las Trampas have a cluster of houses around a plaza as well as other houses scattered along the river. The tendency in this century has been toward highway and road orientation which now predominates in Santa Cruz, Truchas, and El Rito, towns which once focused on plazas.

These villages are somewhat isolated because of their small size, the often rugged terrain, and their remoteness from metropolitan areas. Only recently have they had easy communication with other towns and cities. The road between Española and Santa Fe was paved with oil and gravel in 1930. The road from Española to Chimayó was first paved in 1948, and from there on to Truchas, Las Trampas, and Peñasco in 1954. State Road 3 to Villanueva was first paved in 1952. Some towns such as Cañones, El Valle, and Cañon Plaza are still accessible only by dirt roads.

The relative isolation of the entire region has allowed these villages to retain some aspects of their Spanish Colonial heritage in spite of their "annexation" by the United States five or six generations ago. The influence of the mainstream United States culture has been limited but ever present during this period, so that today the villages still reflect their Hispanic origin, yet they have incorporated much that is typically American. This cultural duality and merging has given northern New Mexico a particular style in architecture, as well as in language, food, customs, and other cultural aspects. The mountain villages and, to a lesser extent, all of Hispanic New Mexico, have a distinct cultural heritage that has been influenced and altered by American culture rather than overrun by it.

The houses, which are a product of this cultural fusion, have a distinct architectural style different from the Spanish Colonial houses from which they evolved, and different from the typical American house which has been a source of influence for more than a century and a half. These village houses are typically adobe with colored stucco on the exterior, colored plaster on the interior, painted woodwork and trim, and pitched corrugated metal roofs. The form of the house and the architectural details follow certain patterns determined by the age of the house and its general location within the region.

The similar origins and the shared history and circumstances of these villages have allowed them collectively to develop and perpetuate this particular architectural style. Similar houses, which are closely related and have common origins, can be found elsewhere in New Mexico and Colorado, but the central area of northern New Mexico is unquestionably the predominant source.

This particular architectural style is most evident in the house and does not really exist apart from it. The village churches are closely related in materials, in detailing, and to some extent, in form because they typically were built by local people using the familiar materials and techniques of residential construction. However, they are far fewer in number than the houses, and they differ in certain important features including the dramatic evolution of plan associated with the houses. Commercial buildings are scarce. The few stores that can be found in the villages are often as not in a remodeled house or built onto an existing house. Stores which were built as stores were usually constructed by Anglo traders and do not reflect Hispanic traditions. Other structures such as gas stations and mobile homes are part of the American mainstream and are unrelated to the regional style.

Adobe architecture can be found in many parts of the world: Africa, the Middle East, Spain, and Latin America; however, the adobe houses in northern New Mexico are distinctly American. They have evolved naturally in a forthright manner from diverse cultural sources and have become a rich and varied regional style, different from adobe styles elsewhere in the world or those brought here from Spain and Mexico. Their evolution and diversity show a continuing concern for incorporating current fashion into the basic style and for modifying the house for greater comfort and convenience.

These houses have a very different origin from the popular "Santa Fe adobe" and have little in common with it. The Santa Fe style is a self-conscious attempt to recapture a romantic image of old Southwest architecture, both Spanish and Indian. The Santa Fe adobe style, which has all but eliminated any other style in Santa Fe, has been widely used in Taos and Albuquerque as well, and is beginning to make inroads elsewhere in northern New Mexico. Diverse building types such as bungalow-type houses, tract houses, office buildings, theaters, and even gas stations have been built in this style.

Out of enthusiasm for New Mexico's rich cultural heritage and in reaction to the ordinary American building styles that were proliferating in Santa Fe, a group of Santa Fe citizens created the Santa Fe style in the early 1900s. The key elements of the style were (and still are) flat roofs, walls of adobe or at least thick enough to suggest adobe, earth-colored stucco on the exterior and white plaster on the interior, exterior woodwork stained dark brown or painted white, interior woodwork stained, and a set of details including corbels, bancos, corner fireplaces, and portales. The Santa Fe style is unquestionably a legitimate and appealing regional style, but it is very different in origin, intent, and appearance from the adobe houses of rural New Mexico. With its dramatically different look and its high visibility in Santa Fe, Albuquerque, and Taos, the Santa Fe style has completely overshadowed the rural style and is now popularly considered to be the one and only authentic regional adobe style.

While the Santa Fe style continues to be popular, the rural style is sharply on the decline. The tin-roofed adobe houses of the villages were built by their owners with adobe bricks made on the site from the available dirt, peeled pine or spruce logs cut in the mountains nearby, and locally milled lumber. The work was hard but the basic building materials were cheap. Today, the tradition of owner-built houses is still common, but the regional style is disappearing. It is quicker and more practical to use other building materials instead of adobe and vigas. The form of the new houses is typically suburban and mainstream.

The old, and some not so old, houses of the tin-roofed adobe style are still in the majority in most of the small towns of northern New Mexico, but they are quickly disappearing. Many are abandoned because the economic life of the village is so limited that the people have left to find work elsewhere. In some cases the houses are still inhabited but the owners cannot afford the necessary maintenance. In other cases the houses are remodeled in a manner unsympathetic to the original character.

A renewed appreciation for these old-style houses may be emerging within the villages. There adobe has always been favorably regarded as an excellent building material, warm in winter, cool in summer, solid, and reliable. Many people have lamented the constant work required to maintain old adobe houses, but some have acknowledged their special worth. Whether these houses are allowed to deteriorate and collapse over the decades or whether they are discovered, sought after, renovated, and restored, they will never be more numerous, authentic, and unassumingly appealing than they are today.

Figure 1. The first postmaster of Velarde, David Velarde, is said to have built this house. The red-painted roof is more than fifty years old. The walls are white and the wood trim is red and white.

Figure 2. The Cleotilde Abeyta house in Brazos was built in 1914. The roof and portal are part of the original house. There is an **L**-shaped stair to the attic.

Figure 3. This Los Ojos house was built about 1895. The original board
roof was replaced with metal in the 1950s. There are two interior stairs.
The walls are peach colored and the trim is apple green.

Figure 4. This Ojo Caliente house started as a single file of four rooms with a flat roof. The pitched roof was added after the Second World War and has only one cross gable dormer, though many houses in Ojo Caliente have several.

Figure 5. The inset portal of the Sandoval house, with the shingle-covered fascia, is unique in the Truchas area. The gables are also covered in yellow-painted wood shingles. The walls under the portal are light aqua with a white wood wainscot. The roof ladder is a common feature, though most are not so long.

Figure 6. This cottage in Mora has a roof pitch steeper than 45°, which is fairly unusual throughout the region. This galvanized metal roof was painted at some point with aluminum paint. Galvanized roofs are normally left unpainted because paint provides little protection.

Figure 7. The north wall of the Cassidy store in Cleveland near Mora has deteriorated mud plaster which was once painted. The heavy white cornice and the shutters are two common features of Territorial architecture which were not often incorporated into the rural houses. A concrete veneer has been added to the base of the wall for protection against moisture.

Early Spanish Settlements

Spanish explorers first saw the upper Río Grande Valley in 1540. The land was a vast rugged plateau with mountain ranges and broad arid valleys, hot in summer and cold in winter. The land was noticeably similar to the central region of Spain, which was home for many of the New World adventurers. Some areas were rolling grasslands, others rocky and barren, still others were covered with a dark green pygmy forest of oak, pine, or juniper.

Densely populated Indian pueblos were dotted along the Río Grande and in valleys beyond. The drainage areas had stands of cottonwood or willow laced with sandy arroyos and riverbeds made and remade many times by the Río Grande, the Chama, the Ojo Caliente, and their tributaries. These rivers and streams formed a fan-shaped watershed between the Jemez Mountains and the Sangre de Cristos. Here at the conflux of these rivers and in the center of the northern pueblos, the first Spanish colony in New Mexico was established. The year was 1598. Twelve years later, a site on the Santa Fe River was chosen as the new government outpost of the Viceroyalty of New Spain.

The Spanish efforts toward colonization and control of the region in the seventeenth century focused primarily on the domination of the

Pueblo Indians. Spanish friars established many missions at the existing Pueblo villages. There were more than a dozen along the Río Grande from Taos to Socorro and below. About an equal number were scattered to the east and west, mostly within one or two days' journey from the Río Grande missions. This period of colonization ended abruptly when the Indians of many pueblos rose in a single day and massacred several hundred Spaniards. The remaining colonists fled southward along the Río Grande to El Paso del Norte, entirely abandoning the Kingdom of New Mexico.

After the reconquest of the Río Grande Pueblos in 1693, the century of colonization that followed was more independent of the Pueblos. Many of those who accompanied Don Diego de Vargas during the reconquest were colonists from Spanish towns in Mexico who were looking for new lands to farm and graze. Initially, resettlement took place along the Río Grande near the Pueblo sites, but Spanish sites independent of the Pueblo villages soon developed. During this century the Spanish settlements steadily increased in population.

The Spanish settlers required lands along perennial rivers with enough flow for irrigation. In the rugged terrain of the Río Grande Valley and its surrounding mountains, where great gorges, stone outcroppings, sheer faces of rock, steep foothills, and narrow canyons are common, the sites suitable for the Spanish system of irrigation were relatively few and small. By the middle of the eighteenth century the Spanish were pushing at the edges of the Río Grande Valley and elsewhere up the Chama River in search of new lands to cultivate and graze.

Parts of the Santa Cruz Valley, including Chimayó, had been settled before the Revolt of 1680. In 1695, shortly after the reconquest, the town of Santa Cruz was established along the Santa Cruz River just a few miles east of the Río Grande. Houses were continuously connected and faced inward to form a fortress-like structure enclosing a plaza. Chimayó was resettled about the same time.[1] Within a few years other communities and ranchos were established along the river between Santa Cruz and Chimayó. In 1807 Zebulon Montgomery Pike estimated the population of the valley at 2,000.

The lands bordering the lower Chama River began to be settled in the 1730s. The nearby Ojo Caliente area was settled about the same time but was then abandoned until the 1790s, owing to hostilities with the Utes. In the early 1800s settlement was begun along the upper Chama. After decades of petitioning, settlement rights in the Tierra Amarilla area finally were approved in 1832.

Parts of the Embudo watershed were settled by 1740.[2] In 1752 the Las Trampas land grant was given. The Truchas settlement grant was approved in 1754.

The areas to the east of the Sangre de Cristo Mountains were first settled about fifty to one hundred years later than the Río Grande watershed to the west. The eastern frontier areas along the Pecos and to the northeast along the foothills of the Sangre de Cristos were controlled by the Apaches and the Comanches, but pressure for new land opened up the Pecos Valley to settlement despite the Indian danger. In the late 1700s Villanueva began as a walled placita settlement on a bluff overlooking the Pecos River. San Miguel del Vado, a few miles upstream, was settled in 1794 mainly by *genízaros*, Indians living among the Spaniards usually because they had been captured and held by an enemy tribe and were later ransomed by the Spanish. San José was begun in 1803 and Tecolote in 1824. Both Las Vegas and Mora were founded by grants in 1835, although Mora had been settled since 1819.

Shortly after Mexican Independence in 1821, French and American mountain men were trapping throughout the northern mountains, and traders from the United States were making their first cautious visits to the towns of New Mexico. The Hispanic communities on the eastern frontier had frequent contact with Americans and Europeans almost from their beginning. The influence came mostly from commerce with the trappers, the traders, and later the United States Army, but some outsiders married into village families and settled in the region.

With the great success of the Santa Fe Trail in the middle of the nineteenth century, the exposure to the United States increased, especially for Las Vegas, Tecolote, and San Miguel del Vado which were on the trail. The style of architecture in these areas reflects this early influence. The adobe houses of Mora and Las Vegas in particular have certain features rarely found in the Río Grande villages and which suggest early Anglo or French influence.

Figure 8. Stands of cottonwoods in the wide Santa Barbara River Valley near Peñasco, Taos County (elevation 7,500 feet).

Figure 9. Looking northward to the village of Rodarte (elevation 7,500 feet) in the Santa Bárbara River valley, Taos County.

Figure 10. A view of Córdova (elevation 7,000 feet) looking westward across the Río Quemado, Río Arriba County.

Figure 11. Truchas (elevation 8,000 feet) and the Sangre de Cristo Mountains to the east, Río Arriba County.

Figure 12. Villanueva (elevation 6,000 feet) and the valley of the Pecos River beyond, San Miguel County.

Figure 13. Lower Rociada (elevation 7,500 feet) and the eastern foothills of the Sangre de Cristos beyond, San Miguel County.

Figure 14. Los Ojos (elevation 7,500 feet) and the Chama River to the west, Río Arriba County.

The Hispanic Legacy

The village houses of northern New Mexico are made in a simple way from a few ordinary materials. The forms are uncomplicated and the ornamentation is limited. However, these houses have a complex and sophisticated lineage. Most obviously, they are a result of Hispanic house forms merging with common American influences. The Hispanic element is a composite which has links to Rome, North Africa, Christian Spain, and Colonial Mexico. The American element reflects architectural fashion in the United States during the last 150 years.

The Spanish Colonial house of New Mexico has often been described.[1] The walls were adobe brick two or three feet thick; the foundations were usually uncut stone or river rock set in mud mortar. The ceilings were peeled logs covered with poles or hand-split cedar, then branches or straw, with about a foot of dirt on top to form the roof. The walls extended above the roof to create a parapet, which was interrupted occasionally with a wooden waterspout or *canal* to drain the roof. The walls were mud plastered inside and out and covered with homemade whitewash or *jaspe* inside and on outside walls which were protected from rain. The *jaspe* was sometimes tinted with red mud and applied to the outer walls of the houses.[2] The floors were compacted earth and often covered with animal skins or coarse homespun wool carpeting called *jerga*. Corner fireplaces were common, although larger hooded fireplaces were often used for cooking.

The prototypical form of the house was a single line of rooms one story in height all around a square courtyard or *plazuela*, although most houses had too few rooms to enclose a courtyard. Nearly all the rooms of a *plazuela* house had doors onto the courtyard and were protected by covered porches or portales along one or two walls, if not all four. The patio often contained the well and perhaps a few plants.[3] Usually a wide covered opening or zaguán led from the exterior of the house into the courtyard. There were few if any openings on the outside of the house other than the zaguán. Only a few houses facing an important town plaza had portales along the street façade. These served as public arcades. The exterior was stark and boxlike. The rooms were square or rectangular, and usually about thirteen to sixteen feet in the direction of the span of the logs or vigas, normally the shorter dimension of the room. By today's standards the rooms were spacious, with high ceilings, and sparse furnishings. Often the same room served as dining, sitting, and sleeping room. The residents folded mattresses of straw or wool during the day and placed them against the wall for seating, and unfolded them at night for sleeping. The linear form of the house and the simple plan without hallways, closets, and indoor plumbing made the rooms somewhat multipurpose and interchangeable in terms of use. It was common practice to move the kitchen seasonally from one room to another. The rooms, being more or less autonomous and undifferentiated, could be added on or torn down without affecting the spatial organization of the house. The ownership and designated use of a room could be reassigned according to changes within the family. Through inheritance, several contiguous rooms might come to be owned by one family and other rooms owned by a distantly related family. Roland F. Dickey described the way some houses evolved:

> Beginning with a single room, the house grew like a game of dominoes. As each son brought home his bride, he added a room to one end of the paternal dwelling. Every room had its own outside door, and the system solved the in-law problem by giving privacy to the married couples of the family.[4]

All wood was handworked, and hardware was scarce. Interior doorways were often hung with a cloth instead of a wooden door. Clothing, dishes, and other articles were kept in trunks and in niches or cupboards called *alacenas* which were recessed into the thick adobe walls. Mantas were used to conceal the rough vigas and to catch the dirt and dust that sifted down from the roof. Mantas were made of cotton cloth sewn together into a rectangle the size of the room and attached to the walls beneath the vigas (Figure 105).

The rural household was nearly self-sufficient and had various auxiliary structures, which included storerooms, workrooms, animal shelters, and root cellars or *despensas*. A large household might have a separate service patio attached at the rear and enclosed by these rooms and possibly servants' rooms (Figure 25).

The ancient Mediterranean practice of building a house facing inward to a central patio or atrium surrounded by a colonnade probably took root in Spain during the period from about 200 B.C. to 400 A.D. when Spain was a major Roman colony. The Moors who ruled parts of Spain for more than 700 years reinforced the tradition of the courtyard house as a private inward-facing compound. At the end of the fifteenth century when the Moors were expelled from Spain and the New World was discovered, the courtyard house was thoroughly Spanish.

This building form was widely used in Colonial Mexico. For example, the town of Morelia, Michoacán, a prominent Colonial center during the seventeenth and eighteenth centuries, has dozens of courtyard houses and larger buildings built during that era. They are typically two-story stone buildings with a central patio which is slightly sunken, paved with stone, and surrounded by a one- or two-story portal of stone columns and arches.

The Spanish brought the courtyard house with them to New Mexico and found it to be useful as a fortification against Indian raids. However, the courtyard house, which presumes that much of the activity and circulation within the house happens in the courtyard, is not well suited to the colder climate of northern New Mexico. The courtyard is less useful during the cold winters, and the heat lost through exterior walls is greater than for a more compact house plan. Yet this house form, the single file of rooms, persisted into the twentieth century in rural northern New Mexico.

The Spanish colonists evidently built few two-story houses in northern New Mexico, although they were common in both Spain and Mexico. The nearby Pueblo Indians were using adobe to build multistory structures, and the Spanish did build church towers and fortified towers, called torreones, which were several stories tall. However, the typical dirt roof would not be a very satisfactory second floor because the upstairs activity would increase the sifting of dirt down through the sticks or boards into the rooms below. It is also possible that protected outdoor space was so valuable on the frontier that all building efforts were located at ground-level to help form patios.

Rooftops were a part of the household domain, however. Rooftop access was indispensible in order to repair leaks after a heavy rain or snow. Access was often by means of a ladder through a hatchway in the ceiling.[5] Some of the early parapets had battlements because the buildings were defended from the rooftops. The flat rooftops or az-oteas also served as a promenade under better circumstances.[6]

The adobe brick is as old as the great civilizations of Mesopotamia and has been widely used throughout the Mediterranean region for thousands of years. The Moors probably brought adobe brick construction to Spain from North Africa in the eighth century A.D. because the word *adobe* is Arabic in origin. The Spanish brought the technique to the Americas where it has been widely used. The Pueblo Indians were building with earth before the arrival of the Spanish, but they were using pressed handfuls of damp clay rather than the dried adobe brick.

The plain wood ceilings with exposed beams are typical of Christian Spain, although the few examples in New Mexico of beams that are carved and worked with touches of colored paint show Moorish influence. The use of wooden poles, called *latillas*, placed side by side to span between the vigas, was borrowed from the Pueblo Indians. Important rooms of early Hispanic houses sometimes had a ceiling of latillas laid in a herringbone pattern and painted red, blue, or green.[7]

Terra cotta tile, so abundant in Spain and Mexico, evidently was never used in New Mexico. However, it would have been a great improvement over adobe for both floors and roofs. The reason may be that no large, uniform, and readily accessible source of clay existed in New Mexico. Good clay was found in many places but in such limited quantity that its use for floor and roof tiles may not have been practical.

The masonry arch, vault, and dome were also very common in Spain and Mexico but were not used here beyond one or two instances. Timber for roof framing was plentiful in New Mexico and provided a quicker method of roofing or bridging a wall opening. It was a technique familiar to Indian laborers who were employed for much of the early Spanish construction.

The tradition of plastered and whitewashed interior walls is common to both Spain and Mexico. Whitewashed exterior walls are popular in southern Spain and parts of Mexico. The painted dado or band of color along the base of the wall to a height of several feet is still a common sight in Spain and is used without restraint in Mexico. The dado is normally darker than the wall and helps hide dirt spattered from the street or the ground. In New Mexico a dado of *tierra amarilla*, a yellow clay wash with small flakes of mica, was sometimes painted on interior walls or walls under a portal.

The Spanish Colonial house of New Mexico, although constructed with a considerably more limited range of building materials and architectural details, retained many of the same basic architectural qualities as its antecedents in Mexico and in Christian and Moorish Spain. It was characteristically Hispanic in its single line of rooms enclosing a courtyard or aspiring to do so, and in its thick masonry walls covered with plaster. Beyond this, the house had a tendency toward monumentality. This characteristic was apparent in the often long expanse of thick adobe walls interrupted only occasionally by simple doors and windows. Often the ceilings were high, perhaps ten feet, giving the house a larger scale both inside and out. The portales were continuous along entire façades and generally tall, eight or nine feet to the lintel. The scale of these basic elements was increased further by the lack of fussy details.

The simple floor plan, consisting of a series of spacious, well-proportioned rooms without the complexity of halls, closets, and bathrooms also contributed to the effect. This simple, understated monumentality is also characteristic of the architecture of Mexico and Spain, and is more fundamental to its appeal than the architectural details that have been so abundantly copied.

The Spanish Colonial house of New Mexico has been carried forward to the twentieth century, and has been radically transformed over the years to accept new influences, changing requirements, and modern materials and techniques. Nearly all these transformations have occurred since the arrival of the United States Army in 1846. Thus began the period of upheaval and rapid change of the colonial way of life in New Mexico.

Figure 15. The zaguán of the Manuel Romero house in Las Vegas and the courtyard beyond are among the few remaining examples of what were once common features of Spanish Colonial houses in New Mexico.

Figure 16. This abandoned Chimayó adobe has the features and proportions of an old house. The roof, too, appears to have been built before the First World War. The roof is very rusted, and the walls are mud plastered.

Figure 17. The Archuleta house in Truchas, which turns a blank south wall to the street, recalls earlier days in Truchas when houses turned inward with few doors and windows facing the street.

Figure 18. The portal and entry of the Archuleta house in Truchas face north away from the road. The roof line of the porch has been changed, probably to reduce snow buildup. An exterior stair to a gable door can be seen on the right.

Figure 19. These joined houses form the east side of the Plaza del Cerro in Chimayó. The triangular pediments and the transoms suggest that the buildings were owned by people of means during the nineteenth century.

Figure 20. This old house on the south side of the Plaza del Cerro in Chimayó was the first on the plaza to receive a pitched roof. Children would sleep up there under the metal roof on summer nights. The walls are peach-colored stucco. The woodwork is white with red screen doors. A concrete veneer protects the base of the wall.

Figure 21. The Tafoya house in Truchas is a classic example of early pitched roof adobes. It has a large scale rarely seen in later houses. The single file of rooms is placed right at the street edge. The Romero house, which has been torn down, was originally connected at the right, forming a continuous façade.

Figure 22. A painted dado without a portal is rare. This house near Holman in Mora County has a green dado on white walls.

Yankee Newcomers

When American travelers first sighted New Mexican towns in the early and mid 1800s, they compared them to brickyards or river barges. Probably this description was derived as much from the lack of landscaping as from the single-story flat-roofed adobe buildings. The following account by Matthew C. Field, which appeared in a New Orleans newspaper in 1840, is one of the more positive first impressions of Santa Fe by a traveler from the United States:

> We had wasted a few days in the Toas [sic] valley
> before we paid our visit to Santa Fe, consequently our
> first view of the mud built city was from the mountain
> side, as we descended after crossing from the distant
> valley. There, within half a mile of the base of the
> mountain, a small spot of the vast green plain that
> spread away before us was dotted with low one story
> buildings, reminding us irresistably [sic] of an
> assemblage of mole hills. As we approached the city
> and the houses began to shape themselves more
> distinctly to the eye, the church in the centre, soaring
> above the surrounding dwellings, attracted our
> attention. It was built as high and quite as large as any
> of our ordinary sized meeting houses, and upon after

43

[sic] examination our surprise was not a little excited to find that these mud walls could possess such strength and durability. It would be perfectly practicable for the inhabitants to build their houses two or more stories high as far as strong walls are necessary for that purpose, and the reason why they are not so built is not, as one would at first imagine, because mud walls are inefficient, but because ground is cheap, and the people prefer half a dozen rooms in a row to as many apartments piled one above another. They think it is easier to go through a door way than up a pair of stairs, which is certainly not a very unreasonable conclusion to arrive at. Besides, although timber is plenty carpenters are scarce, and a boarded floor is a luxury for which they entertain not the slightest ambition.

The apartments are of various lengths but never exceeding twenty feet in width, (the church alone is an exception,) and across the walls from side to side are stretched, sometimes good hewn timber, sometimes rude branches, according to the means of the builder. Over these is laid a thick covering of grass and straw, and upon this earth is piled from one to two feet deep, which forms the roof. A very pleasing effect is produced by the grass growing on the tops of the houses, and as all the dwellings are connected it is not uncommon to see children chasing each other the whole length of a street along the house tops.[1]

In 1821, when Mexican Independence ended Spain's policy of closed borders, Frenchmen and Americans began trapping beaver throughout the remote mountain areas of New Mexico. The foreigners often had homes in Santa Fe or Taos, and some became Mexican citizens. The Santa Fe Trail was established as a trade route during the same period. American traders opened mercantile stores on the Santa Fe plaza during the 1830s. About forty foreigners lived in Santa Fe then, about twenty of whom were naturalized citizens.[2] The first two-story businesses on the plaza were built by Anglos between 1846 and 1849.[3]

The first pitched roof building in Santa Fe may have been the "Casa Americana" built by Louis Dorrance in 1850 and bought by Bishop Lamy a few years later to be used as his residence. The building had a simple gable roof with wood shingles and a two-story porch across the front. It was dubbed "Casa Americana" by the local population because it represented a new architectural style imported by the Americans.[4]

Throughout the region, Europeans as well as Americans were doing business of one sort or another in ever-increasing numbers. They were the first to influence the traditional colonial architecture in New Mexico, although their impact was minor compared to that of the United States Army.

The United States conquest of the Spanish Southwest brought many more Anglos to New Mexico. The U.S. soldiers were a highly visible presence after 1846 and were among the first to introduce new types of building materials and to construct American-style buildings in the New Mexican Territory. The U.S. Army constructed the first sawmill near Santa Fe in 1847. Other sawmills followed, and lumber soon became more widely available.

Initially the U.S. forts were flat-roofed adobe structures which incorporated only minor imported materials including nails, some hardware, and glass.[5] Some of these early forts had single-story Greek Revival porches along the entire front of the building. As army activities expanded in New Mexico, the forts became larger and more elaborate. By 1859 Fort Union had at least a dozen pitched-roof buildings. The officers' quarters of Fort Marcy, which was just to the north of the Santa Fe plaza, were among the most highly visible examples of a completely American-style house, except that adobe was used for the walls (Figure

23). They were constructed in the early 1870s using a compact two-story plan which was symmetrical except for a service wing at the rear. The pitched roof was covered with flat metal sheets with standing seams. The house had large white double-hung windows and a simple white porch with square columns running the entire length of the façade. The front door, with its transom and side lights, opened into a central hall. The thick window and door openings were splayed and cased with wood panels. The house was Georgian in plan with simple Greek Revival details.

As the military expanded in New Mexico the number of American carpenters increased. In 1861 Father John B. Salpointe directed the construction of a new board-and-wood-shingle pitched roof for the little adobe church at Mora, which until then had been covered with a flat dirt roof. In reference to this project, he remarked, "As to the carpenter work, it was generally done with less difficulty, as there were already in the country American carpenters who understood their trade well enough to make doors and windows, and to cover a building."[6]

North of Mora, Lucien Maxwell was establishing his empire. His first great house, built at Rayado, was a single-story, flat-roofed courtyard house. The second great house was built at Cimarrón in about 1857. It was adobe, two stories high, with pitched roofs, dormer and bay windows, wide verandas, front balustrade, and a white picket fence. This house may have been one of the earliest of the American-style houses in northern New Mexico.

Along the Chama River at Los Ojos (later called Parkview), an entrepreneur from Wisconsin named Thomas Burns built a two-story adobe with a steep gabled roof and dormer windows. This house served as a prototype for a series of similar houses in the Tierra Amarilla area which were built or remodeled in the 1870s.[7]

By the early 1880s the buildings in Santa Fe and Las Vegas were beginning to display Victorian styles. The new rail service provided easy transportation for new building materials, including filigree brackets, turned columns, molded metal work, and so on. Sheet metal for roofing also arrived by rail. On March 19, 1882, in Santa Fe, Adolph Bandelier noted in his journal the changes that had taken place in the city since he was last there in December 1880. He wrote, "The city has grown considerably. New houses have sprung up, some two-story, of stone and brick, some one story of adobe, with metallic roofs. The latter houses are very fine and good-looking."

The twenty-year period following the Civil War brought many new American-style buildings to northern New Mexico. By the time the railroad arrived, or shortly thereafter, there were numerous examples of Greek Revival buildings and later Victorian styles, too. Most of these were in Santa Fe and Las Vegas, but others were scattered throughout the territory and provided an irresistible influence for the Hispanic building traditions.

Birth of a Style

Although many of the citizens of New Mexico were not happy with the American annexation of their homeland, American fashion was adopted fairly quickly in the areas where there was much trade and communication with Anglos. W. W. H. Davis reported that Santa Fe women attending a local dance in 1853 were in American-style dress. In 1866 James F. Meline wrote, "In nothing has American influence so strongly shown itself as in the changed and changing dress of both men and women in New Mexico." Fray Angélico Chávez has also mentioned how avidly New Mexicans wanted to become American.[1] There seems to have been little resistance to American culture, at least in superficial aspects such as dress and architectural details.

During the period of the 1850s through the 1870s in Santa Fe, Las Vegas, and other prosperous towns, the adobe houses were being "dressed up" with new white American-style woodwork, including neoclassic front porches with square tapered columns, doors and double-hung windows cased with milled lumber and capped with classic pediments, balustrades between the porch columns, and perhaps a picket fence outlining a front yard.

Hispanic Colonial houses were typically placed at the very edge of the street but faced inward toward the courtyard. American-style houses were set back from the street but were front-facing and street-oriented. The original orientation of the old adobes was somewhat altered by the application of the rather formal and symmetrical white woodwork of the front façade. The white picket fence around the front yard was another radical change. Instead of the enclosed private courtyard invisible from the street, the front yard was visible, accessible, and more public than private. It was almost as if the Hispanic courtyard house had been turned inside out.

Although the compact street-oriented nature of the American-style house was the very opposite of the colonial adobe, there were certain similarities of style and proportion. The neoclassic quality of the American house had the same Mediterranean origin as the Hispanic house. Both the white neoclassic porch and the Spanish Colonial portal were derived from the classical Mediterranean peristyle. The monumentality of the Spanish Colonial house, with its spacious well-proportioned rooms, had much in common with American neoclassicism, which achieved monumentality by using large simple geometric forms and oversized architectural elements. The front door, the focal point of the façade, was often compounded with side lights and a transom in order to create a larger architectural element. Windows also were large, and ceilings were high.

When the neoclassic details were incorporated into a colonial adobe, the results were immediately successful, due to the classical nature of the two styles. The difference in the internal organization of the two house types was far more difficult to resolve and required generations to reach some sort of equilibrium. The single front door, the entrance hall, the two-story plan, the symmetrical façade, and later the interior plumbing, the closets, and the hallways were all incorporated, usually piecemeal and often in very individualistic ways, into the original Hispanic house type. Some of the adaptations were more successful and more widely used than others. For example, the second-story plan was loosely transformed into an attic space with dormer or gable windows. This has become a very successful and characteristic feature of Hispanic houses in New Mexico.

On the other hand, the single front door was incompatible with the single file of more or less equal rooms each with its own exterior door. It worked well enough for a two-room cottage, which is a common house-type in the town of Mora (Figure 6). It also worked for a courtyard house because the zaguán entry could be transformed into the Territorial front door without affecting the circulation pattern within the house. But for the majority of houses which had a number of rooms in a straight line, or L or U shape, the single front door was unsatisfactory. It became common only as the compact floor plan became common.

Beyond fashion, American building materials and techniques provided solutions to some age-old problems of the Hispanic Colonial house. At the beginning of the American occupation in 1846, only a few buildings in the territory had glass windows. Large, double-hung windows with panes of clear glass must have been eagerly received when they first appeared in the territory. After centuries of repairing leaky mud roofs, the Hispanic population must have been envious of the pitched roofs covered with cedar shingles or standing seam terneplate (80 percent lead, 20 percent tin).

A few picket huts and pine clapboard roofs could be found at distant mining outposts and ranchos during the Mexican period,[2] but there were no pitched-roof houses in the region until a few years after 1846 when terneplate, carried over the Santa Fe Trail, and lumber from local sawmills was available, as well as more sophisticated carpentry tools for making wood shingles. The expense of such materials prohibited their use by the average rural homeowner. The railroad, which first reached New Mexico in 1879, brought corrugated iron, lowering the price of a pitched metal roof considerably, but it was still unaffordable for most rural farmers and ranchers operating in a barter economy.

Lime plaster was made near Fort Union before the Civil War and stucco (cement plaster with lime) was used in Las Vegas as early as the 1870s.[3] Stucco was brought to New Mexico by rail, but the relatively high cost and, possibly, the unfamiliarity with the techniques of application delayed its widespread use in rural areas until after World War II.

The railroad also brought oil-based paint and wallpaper, as well as architectural woodwork and moldings.[4] These new materials were introduced into the territory over a rather short period of time, yet most rural homeowners could not afford them until much later. The impression made by the early American-style houses was perhaps so vivid that it became a fixed image. The local population continued to aspire to that particular look of pitched metal roofs with gables, long porches, and picket fences painted white and to delight in figured wallpaper and oil-based paint in rich colors.

Brick was first imported to New Mexico in the 1860s, handmade locally in the 1870s, and manufactured on a larger scale after about 1880. Its use in the early Territorial houses was limited to chimneys and parapets. Even though brick houses appeared in Santa Fe and Las Vegas during the railroad era, the use of brick in the rural areas has been confined to chimneys, perhaps because it corresponds to the image of the earliest pitched-roof houses and because the use of adobe was an unshakeable tradition in the rural areas until after World War II. Santa Fe had a few examples of adobe buildings with a cement plaster veneer, scored and painted to look like brick or stone masonry, and at least one adobe building with a fired brick veneer, but such disguises evidently were not used in the rural areas.

Roof dormers were an optional component of the sought-after image. They were a feature of Colonial American architecture of both French and English origin, as well as the later Georgian and Adams styles. Dormers were not particularly characteristic of Greek Revival architecture in the United States although they did sometimes appear on Greek Revival buildings, particularly in the South, as vestiges of an earlier style.

Many of the early Anglo-style houses in Santa Fe had no dormers, including the Casa Americana, the Fort Marcy officers' quarters on Grant and Lincoln avenues, and the Hinojos house on Palace Avenue. However, dormers were a feature of the official residence on Washington Avenue of the commanding officer at Fort Marcy (Figure 23).

The Maxwell Mansion, built in the 1850s in Cimarrón, had a wood-shingle roof with dormer windows which have been attributed to French influence.[5] Baca's Folly, a remarkable three-story structure built in Las Vegas in 1879, also had a wood-shingle roof with dormers.

Dormers returned to fashion in the United States in the early 1900s as part of the prairie style. These were low, wide, hipped-roof dormers set on a compact hipped-roof house. The arrival of this style coincided with a period of relative prosperity in the region which led to the construction of new pitched metal roofs in the rural areas. The influence of the prairie style probably increased the popularity of hipped roofs and dormers throughout the region.

In Santa Fe, Albuquerque, and to a lesser extent Taos and Española, the Anglo presence has been so strong that the Hispanic house type with its American adaptations has been outnumbered and overwhelmed by purely Anglo-style houses. In Santa Fe, Taos, and Albuquerque, the universal popularity of the Santa Fe style has somewhat obscured what distinctions remained among house types. The economic stagnation in Las Vegas during this century has preserved a number of adapted houses of Hispanic origin. In the smaller and more remote villages of northern New Mexico, the evolution of the Hispanic house has continued in its own way and has created a dynamic and distinct style with many variations both regional and chronological.

Figure 23. The Fort Marcy commanding officer's quarters on Washington Avenue in Santa Fe was built in the early 1870s. It was among the most important of the early American-style houses built in northern New Mexico, and served as a model for architectural innovation throughout the region. It later became the residence of Governor Miguel A. Otero, Jr. This photograph was taken in the 1890s during that period. (Courtesy Museum of New Mexico).

Figure 24. The Gallegos house in Villanueva is one of the few courtyard houses remaining in northern New Mexico. Two of the unused rooms still have manta ceilings. Another room was once the weaving room and still has walls covered in *yeso* and *tierra amarilla*. Other unused rooms have wallpaper applied directly over mud plaster.

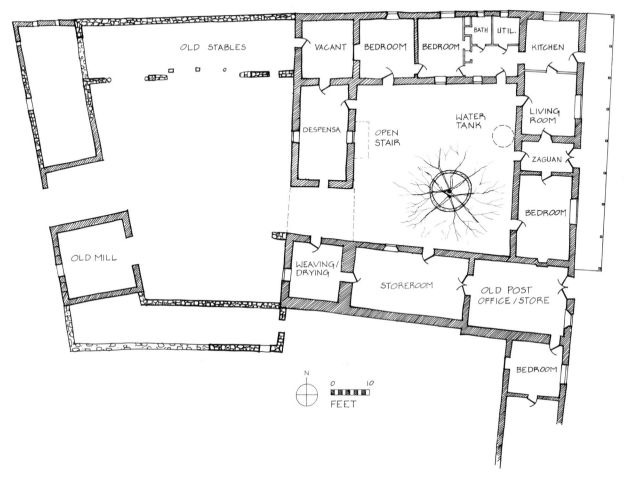

Figure 25. The plan of the Gallegos house shows various modifications which have been made to the house, including wood frame partitions, large wood windows replacing smaller ones in the front wall under the portal, and the removal of the open stairs and water tank in the courtyard. The stair led through a gable doorway into the attic. The water tank collected water from the roof by means of gutters. Water for domestic use was carried from the acequia until the community well was dug.

57

Figure 26. The oldest rooms of the Jácquez house in Salazar on the Cañones Creek (Río Arriba County) were built circa 1840. The pitched roof was added in 1907. The ceilings once were ornate pressed metal.

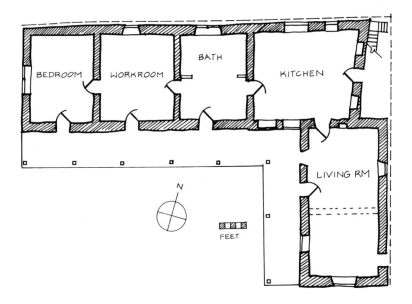

Figure 27. The floor plan of the Jácquez house has a typical arrangement of rooms. One interior adobe wall has been removed and several windows and doors have been added or altered in the kitchen and living room.

Figure 28. The Felipe Valdez house in Los Brazos has a gable balcony and stair which are common in the area. Turquoise and white are used for the walls and the woodwork. The house was built before 1905. The pitched roof was covered with boards until about 1957 when the corrugated metal was added.

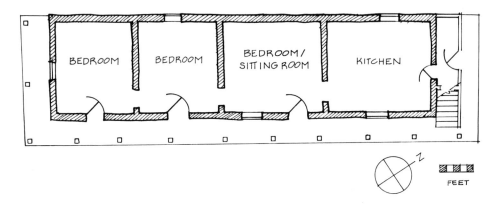

BEDROOM   BEDROOM   BEDROOM/ SITTING ROOM   KITCHEN

FEET

Figure 29.   The plan is a typical single file of rooms. The interior doorways are offset in the walls, although such doorways are usually centered. The common pattern of one window and one door per room is consistent except for the room next to the exterior stair. The low sill of the window under the portal suggests that the opening was once a door.

Figure 30. The Hernández house on the east bank of the Chama River above Abiquiu has a simple gable roof without dormers. The house faces southward to the river and turns its back to the highway.

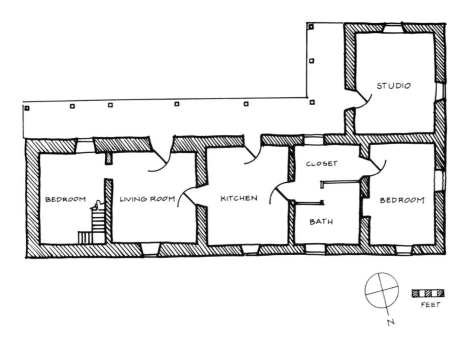

STUDIO

CLOSET

BEDROOM

LIVING ROOM

KITCHEN

BEDROOM

BATH

FEET

N

Figure 31. The Hernández house near Abiquiu has a common **L**-shaped plan with a single file of rooms. The steep narrow staircase is enclosed with boards.

Figure 32. This abandoned house at Tierra Azul (between Hernández and Abiquiu) is one of the most simplified and distilled examples of the American adobe. Each of the four square rooms has one window, one exterior door, and two communicating doors. This house is a link between Spanish Colonial and American house types.

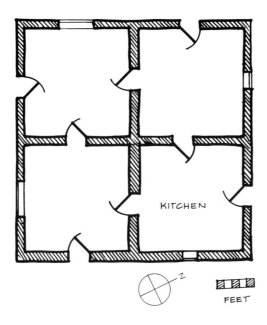

KITCHEN

FEET

Figure 33. The floor plan of the Tierra Azul house is compact but has no central hall. The house has near perfect symmetry of plan but is not the usual bilateral type characteristic of Georgian and Greek Revival styles. The traditional interior circulation pattern of the Hispanic adobe with its line of communicating rooms is maintained despite the compact plan. There is no emphasis on a front façade. A trap door gives access to the attic.

Evolution

In 1914 in the town of Villanueva overlooking the Pecos River, Respicia Gonzáles was to be married to Porfirio Gallegos. As a wedding present he offered her the choice of a honeymoon trip to Denver or a new metal roof for the flat-roofed family adobe that would be their home. She chose the pitched metal roof. The corrugated metal, dark with rust, is still in use. The house has remained the Gallegos family home and is one of the very few intact courtyard houses still standing in New Mexico (Figure 24). In addition to the main courtyard, a second service courtyard is attached to the rear which has the crumbling remains of stables, storerooms, and a two-story adobe grist mill. A Territorial double door with a transom opens into an entrance hall, which appears to have been the original zaguán. The street façade is long and handsome, with butter yellow walls and white woodwork. The full-length Territorial portal had a board floor until it was replaced with concrete.

José Abeyta of Brazos in Río Arriba County recounted that his father, whose parents were originally from Abiquiu, helped build the old family adobe next door (Figure 37) when he was a young man around the turn of the century. Indians helped to build the house, trading their labor for a noontime meal. A carpenter from Denver came down to construct the pitched roof because the local people did not know how to do it. The house has rough-cut stone foundations, which are fairly uncommon, and thick adobe walls. The medium-pitch gable roof is covered with corrugated metal and has no dormers. The portal has slender turned columns and factory-made Victorian brackets. The four-panel doors under the portal have paneled jambs.

These are two early examples of large pitched-roof houses in a village setting. By contrast, the more typical two-, three-, or four-room adobe was slower to acquire a pitched roof and other modifications due to economic conditions within the villages. In the rural areas of northern New Mexico a barter economy was practiced well into the twentieth century. Most families sustained themselves by small-scale farming and ranching. In about 1880 a few men in the area began working for wages on railroad section gangs. By the 1920s many men routinely left their villages for about six months of the year to work for sheep ranches, mining operations, lumber mills, or the railroad in Colorado and elsewhere, sending their paychecks home. This source of cash no doubt funded many home improvements until the depression when such jobs became scarce. During World War II soldiers from northern New Mexico often sent home pay, which the families used for home improvements. The period of prosperity following the war saw further renovations.

At the turn of the century, the houses of northern New Mexico villages, almost without exception, were flat-roofed, mud-plastered buildings without portales. They were heated by wood, lit by candles or kerosene lamps, and had no indoor plumbing. In 1935, when the Tewa Basin Study[1] was conducted, conditions were much the same throughout the region, although pitched roofs were becoming more common, and some portales could be seen. The study reported that houses at Cundiyo were plastered with white clay and had flat roofs except for four pitched-roof houses. The houses at Ojo Sarco were plastered with white clay and those at Truchas with dark grey clay. The houses at Río Chamita were three or four rooms in size, mostly with stone or adobe floors, and ceilings of vigas and juniper limbs.

For a time the two Catholic churches in Canjilón were the only buildings in that village to have pitched metal roofs. In 1935 there was a heavy rain that lasted for days, washing away the mud roofs and flooding the houses of the village. Nearly everyone took refuge in the churches, whose metal roofs withstood the deluge.[2]

A few more prosperous villages had numerous pitched roofs well before the depression. These included Mora, Española, Chimayó, Tierra Amarilla, Brazos, and Los Ojos. Roofs in Mora apparently were flat in 1866,[3] but, by the turn of the century or shortly thereafter, most buildings had pitched roofs. The first pitched roof in Chimayó was built by Epifanio Jaramillo in 1902. The roof is an L-shaped gable roof without dormers and until 1984 was covered with the original corrugated metal which had rusted to a deep purplish brown. H. M. Jaramillo built the next pitched roof on his house the following year. In 1907 a metal roof was added to the Ortega house near Chimayó's old Plaza del Cerro. In 1910 the house on the south side of the plaza acquired a metal roof, and others followed within the decade.[4]

Like the pitched roof, the portal was often an added element rather than part of the original house. A common pattern was the addition of a pitched roof onto an existing flat-roofed house followed by the addition of the portal ten or twenty years later.

Such major alterations made to an existing house are indicative of the attitude that the house is not a balanced and completed design but rather a collection of elements that can be added or subtracted at will. Many houses in existence today in northern New Mexico used to be larger, but certain rooms or sections were "thrown down." Other houses have grown in stages so that different rooms have different ages.

The rooms were built as the need arose and as the means were available. Mercedes Trujillo of Chimayó recounted that when she was young she and her mother used to make adobes in the spring and build a new room in the summer because they wanted a bigger house. The owner-as-builder method of construction encourages this approach. The Spanish Colonial flat-roofed adobe with its single file of rooms is also well suited to the addition of one room at a time. The pitched roof and compact floor plan have made the practice more difficult. Complicated and awkward roof configurations sometimes result from adding onto pitched-roof houses.

Adjacent rooms of old adobe houses often have different floor heights as a result of being built at different times. It is common for the door between adjoining rooms to have a high (as much as nine inches above the floor) wooden threshold the full depth of the common wall.

Other technological improvements were incorporated into most rural houses when the family could afford them. This was usually much later, on the average perhaps fifty or sixty years later, than when the improvement first became available in New Mexico. Board floors were among the earliest modernizations to be incorporated into the Spanish Colonial house type, yet a few rural houses today have sheet linoleum laid directly on top of dirt floors. Cement plaster or stucco on exterior walls became predominant in the rural areas as families acquired the means to buy the necessary materials.

Today virtually all of the rural houses have pitched roofs. Probably about 95 percent have cement plaster, although some lack a final color coat. Most old houses which are still inhabited have a concrete veneer at the base of the exterior walls to protect against moisture (Figure 20). Nearly all of the old corner fireplaces have been removed. The common method of heating is by a space heater of some sort, whether wood-burning, electric, or propane-fueled.

Most of these early modifications in the Spanish Colonial house type consisted of new materials or structures applied over the existing adobe house. These included board floors, cement plaster, portales, pitched roofs, fiberboard ceiling panels, and concrete protection veneers. This phenomenon of the traditional adobe house as a core or base, with the other innovations applied to the surfaces, is characteristic even of new houses built at a time when the technological improvements might have been incorporated into the structure itself.

Houses originally built with pitched roofs nearly always had the traditional mud roof over the vigas anyway, and often had no access to the attic space except by a little door in the gable end which required a ladder. The space under the pitched roof was almost never incorporated into the living space of the house. Because the roof of the attic was sheet steel left exposed on the underside, the dirt floor of the attic was essential as a thermal barrier to protect the house from the extreme heat and cold of the attic. Its importance as insulation was mentioned by several homeowners.

Vigas were still being laid in some new houses in the thirties although milled lumber would have provided a more level surface for attaching the panel and batten ceiling. For a long time the alterations to the Spanish Colonial house were essentially superficial. The applied elements made the house look quite different, but in essence it was much the same.

Apart from the custom of altering a particular house over time, changes have occurred in the rural New Mexican house type itself during the past one hundred years, as the house has evolved from Spanish Colonial toward mainstream American, and as it has followed broad patterns in American architectural fashion. The following table summarizes the evolution of the general form of the house and its major elements:

Aspect	Older Characteristic	More Recent
Wall thickness	Thick (18″–30″)	Thinner (12″–18″)
Wall height	High (11′–12′)	Lower (9′–10′)
Roof pitch	Steep (35°–45°)	Flatter (20°–30°)
Roof type	Gable	Hip
Floor plan	Linear	Compact
Dormer windows	Tall and narrow	Shorter, more square
Dormer roof	Gable	Hip or shed
Window shape	Tall and narrow	Square or horizontal
Window and door trim	Pedimented, three-dimensional	Simplified, flat
Portal	Long	Shorter, smaller

These changes consistently represent a general reduction in scale and extension. The house has become more compact in both plan and elevation. Individual elements such as doors, windows, and dormers have become simpler and less distinguished. This phenomenon is not unique to these New Mexican adobes but seems to follow a general architectural trend in the United States.

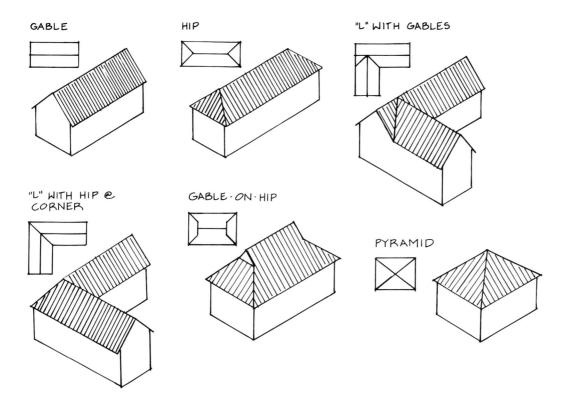

GABLE

HIP

"L" WITH GABLES

"L" WITH HIP e CORNER

GABLE·ON·HIP

PYRAMID

Figure 34. COMMON ROOF FORMS These are the basic roof forms found in the region and are generally arranged from most to least common. A few additional ones exist such as the gambrel and the shed roof but are quite rare. Flat roofs are all but unknown in northern New Mexico except in areas dominated or influenced by the Santa Fe style and in the Pueblo Indian villages.

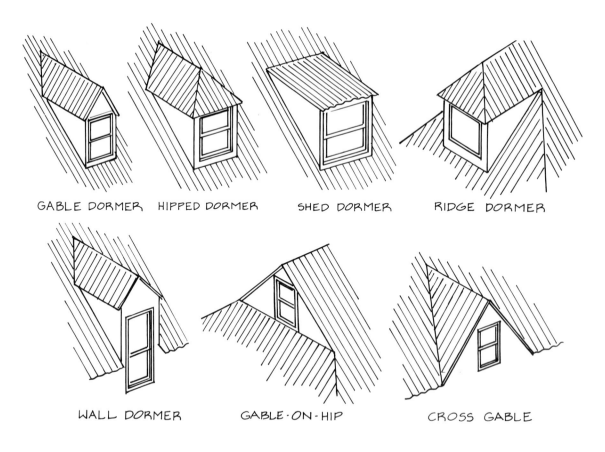

GABLE DORMER   HIPPED DORMER   SHED DORMER   RIDGE DORMER

WALL DORMER   GABLE·ON·HIP   CROSS GABLE

Figure 35. DORMERS AND ATTIC WINDOWS: Dormers are one of the most expressive elements of the rural adobe style, although less than half the rural houses have dormers. The gable dormer is among the oldest of the various dormer types. The hipped dormer is often seen on compact houses with hipped or pyramid-shaped roofs. The shed dormer is also fairly common. The ridge dormer is primarily a local theme in the Chimayó area. The wall dormer is also an old style in northern New Mexico. The gable-on-hip roof window appears most often on compact houses of relatively recent vintage. The cross gable is particularly popular in Ojo Caliente.

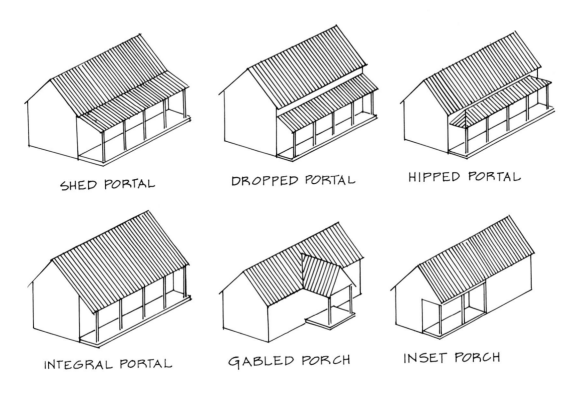

SHED PORTAL DROPPED PORTAL HIPPED PORTAL

INTEGRAL PORTAL GABLED PORCH INSET PORCH

Figure 36. PORTALES AND PORCHES Portales are an important feature of rural adobe houses. The shed portal is quite common in nearly all of the communities. The dropped portal is common in the Tierra Amarilla area. The hipped portal is seen occasionally throughout the region. The integral portal is fairly unusual. The gabled porch is popular in the Mora area. The inset porch is a more recent development associated with compact floor plans.

75

Figure 37. The abandoned Abeyta house in Brazos has large vigas, the ends of which can be seen along the south wall. The brick chimneys and the large scale of the house also ⸍ᵍᵍest that the house is relatively old. Brick chimneys tend to be centere ⸍ ᵃ ⸍ ⸍se are, and never occur on an end wall.

Figure 38. This Truchas house was built in the 1930s by nineteen-year-old Elisa Pacheco and her uncle while her husband was working in Colorado.

Figure 39. The Valdez house in Cleveland was built before 1885, although the pitched roof was added in the early 1970s, replacing the flat dirt roof. The symmetry of the façade is common in the Mora Valley. The Territorial doorway opens into an entrance hall.

Figure 40. This hipped-roof house in Mora has a façade that is as symmetrical as its plan of four equal rooms will allow. The central porch-covered doorway flanked by symmetrical windows is a common arrangement in the Mora valley.

Figure 41. This Chimayó house was built in 1915 with the pitched roof, carriage garage, and hand-made doors. The ladder was used to enter the attic through the gable door. The melting snow on the metal roof shows the spacing of the rafters and purlins.

Figure 42. This uninhabited three-room house in Las Trampas was built in the early 1920s. The roof and portal were added the following year. The exterior is mud plaster painted green under the portal. The ceilings are covered with mantas.

Figure 43.   The Martinez house in Velarde has a roof shape that was popular in Midwestern towns just before World War I. The brick chimneys and the wood shingles painted red also suggest that the roof is about sixty-five years old.

Figure 44. This **U**-shaped adobe in Sapello used to have a board roof and an old portal until they were replaced by a new portal and metal roof in 1962. The portal runs along the three sides of the house that enclose the patio. The double doors and big windows at the gable end suggest that this wing was once a store.

Figure 45. The Martínez house in Brazos was built before 1900. In 1926 the metal roof was put on, replacing the earlier wood shingles. The portal was added in the same year or perhaps earlier. There are five rooms upstairs. The house used to be **T**-shaped and was shared by several families.

Figure 46. The Trujillo house in Córdova is said to be 200 years old. The present portal was built in about 1913, replacing an earlier portal of peeled log columns. The ceiling in one of the rooms has a manta of figured cloth.

Figure 47. The López house in Córdova was built with its pitched roof and portal in about 1935 by the woodcarver Ricardo López. The **L** shape with the gable roof, shed dormers, and continuous portal is typical in Córdova and nearby villages. The aspen logs used by the Cordova woodcarvers are sometimes dried in the attics of the houses.

Figure 48.　This little house in Ojo Sarco was built around 1920. The portal bench is a typical feature. The scalloped fascia board of the portal has two scallops per post. One scallop per post is more common, as used on the Trujillo and López houses in Córdova. The scalloped fascia board was the simplest way of achieving the conceptual profile of the popular brackets at the top of the portal columns.

Figure 49. The symmetrical cross-shaped plan of this Peñasco house is unusual. The roof is more steeply pitched than most. Unlike the typical rural adobe, this house is rented rather than owner-occupied.

Figure 50. This compact adobe was built in Wagon Mound in the early 1900s by the Martínez family. The homemade white lattice work on the porch suggests Victorian filigree.

Figure 51. The Faucett house in Santa Fe is one of the few remaining houses there that have not undergone Santa Fe style remodeling to some degree or other. The house was built in about 1885, but the pitched roof was added later. There is no stair to the attic, and the only access is through the dormer window. The walls are butter yellow stucco with white classic Territorial woodwork. The symmetrical facade is a feature of Territorial rather than Spanish Colonial architecture.

Fundamentals of the Rural Adobe

Although there are regional variations and a chronological development within the style, a number of general characteristics persist. Despite the richness of the variations, these characteristics are dominant and consistent throughout the region. The following characteristics are fundamental to the traditional rural houses of northern New Mexico:

1. The houses are constructed of adobe.

Typically the adobes were made on the site by the family. A Santa Fe house which was built by the owner's family in 1900 was recently remodeled, exposing the original adobes which had been made on the site. Some of the adobes were marked with the hoofprints of deer who had come down from the mountains in the early spring to nibble the straw in the freshly made adobe bricks.

Concrete block has been used as a substitute for adobe in recent years, although adobe is still regarded as an excellent building material. In one instance, a Santa Fe owner/builder constructed walls with concrete block and filled all the cells of the block with dirt.

A few houses, particularly in the poorer villages, are constructed of upright wooden poles chinked and plastered with mud. This type of construction is known as jacal and is considered inferior to solid adobe.

2. The exterior walls are stuccoed in a pastel tint or white.

Fifty years ago most rural houses were still mud plastered. Since that time, stucco (cement plaster) has become the typical exterior finish, although mud plaster can still be seen, usually on abandoned buildings (Figure 7).

Mud plaster painted with ordinary house paint can occasionally be found under a portal.

The final coat of stucco has integral color and is more expensive than the grey undercoats. Some houses lack this final color coat, probably because of the expense. Others have a painted finish in lieu of the color coat. The most commonly used colors are white, cream, yellow, ochre, peach, salmon, green and aqua. Pink and light blue are less common, and lavender is very rare. Brown is the predominant color in Truchas, but is rarely used elsewhere except on recently renovated houses located within the growing sphere of influence of the Santa Fe style.

It seems that shades of green, blue, and aqua are used more frequently in the warmer, drier lowlands, and that warm colors are used more often in the cool, wetter mountain areas, although the distinction, if it does exist, is subtle. However, there is a noticeably predominant use of green in the rocky, red-earthed valley of the Pecos River south of the Sangre de Cristo Mountains.

3. The exterior woodwork is painted in a contrasting color.

White continues to be the most frequent choice of color, although shades of blue, green, yellow, orange, and red are common. Two-toned woodwork is popular throughout the region. White is generally used as the predominant color, with green, blue, yellow, orange, or red used as an accent on the recessed panels of the doors, the wood frames of the door and window screens, and the portal columns. White with green accents seems to be the most popular combination, perhaps because some of the early Territorial houses, including the officers' quarters at Fort Marcy and Fort Union, had white woodwork with green shutters, standard U.S. Army practice at the time.[1]

Today in southern Spain the woodwork and trim are always painted deep green, but in medieval Spain blue was frequently used by the Muslims because it was considered a protection against evil.[2] The popularity of blue woodwork in Santa Fe has been similarly attributed to its protective powers because it is the color of the Virgin's cloak.[3]

The Peñasco area has a few examples of tri-color woodwork, generally using white as a base color with two accent colors.

4. The roof is pitched, corrugated, galvanized steel.

Nearly all the metal roofs in the rural areas of the region are corrugated galvanized steel, although rare examples of standing seam metal roofs do exist. Corrugated metal roofing was introduced in New Mexico after the arrival of the railroad and has been readily available and relatively inexpensive throughout this century. Its application requires no special tools and skills. Mineral-coated asphalt roll roofing (tar paper) occasionally was used, but it deteriorates quickly. Board roofs with battened joints running parallel to the pitch of the roof have also been used. A few abandoned barns still have such roofs.

Many of the early pitched roof houses in the region were covered with cedar shingles. They were watertight if well maintained, but were flammable. Quite a few wood shingle roofs still exist in Las Vegas. Ocate, and elsewhere on the east side of the Sangre de Cristos.

5. The base of the exterior walls has a concrete veneer to protect the adobe at grade from moisture.

Adobe houses traditionally have been built on foundations of rock with mud mortar. Moisture at the base of exterior walls can seriously undermine the integrity of an adobe structure. Typically a concrete veneer is cast at the base of the wall to protect it from moisture. The average size is about six inches wide and about ten inches above grade (Figures 20 and 21). The residents of Las Vegas and the villages along the Pecos River sometimes add a veneer of local flagstone instead of cast concrete.

6. The houses are a single story.

The single-story house is a legacy of the Spanish Colonial era. The difficulty of building and maintaining two-story adobe walls probably contributed to the continued dominance of the single-story house. Two-story houses are less rare in the Chama River basin, particularly at El Rito and Tierra Amarilla. A two-story house type was developed in the Watrous and Wagon Mound area around 1900. Mora, too, has a few two-story houses, and other isolated examples are scattered throughout the region.

7. The attic space is uninsulated and unfinished.

The attic is used for storage and for drying fruit, chiles, corn, and meat. The attic space is framed with poles or milled lumber rafters with collar ties about one or two feet below the ridge. The rafters are spanned with boards every two or three feet. The corrugated steel spans between the boards and is exposed on the underside (Figures 91 and 99). The attic space is usually tall enough to walk around without stooping and is adequately lit by dormer or gable windows. The floor may be compacted earth, boards, or even concrete. The attic space, being cold in winter and hot in summer, is not inhabited, although children sometimes play there or sleep there on summer nights.

8.   Windows are set at the exterior face of the wall with the jambs splayed to the interior; doors are recessed from the exterior face, and the jambs often splay outward.

Splayed window jambs were common in American architecture during the Greek Revival period. They had recessed panels and were painted white. The windows of rural adobes followed this precedent, although the jambs were usually plain rather than paneled (Figure 90).

The outward splay of the door jambs is another matter. Imported Yankee architecture provided no clear prototype for what became a common exterior doorway of the rural adobe. The doors of the officers' houses at Fort Marcy in Santa Fe were set at the outer edge of the wall with the jambs splayed to the interior in the same manner as the windows. These houses had porches over all three exterior doors, so weathering was not a consideration as it was elsewhere when an exterior door was placed in an unprotected wall. The recessed doorways of the rural adobe (Figure 62), in conjunction with windows set at the opposite face of the wall, have the added, though probably unintentional, esthetic advantage of displaying the thickness of the adobe walls from both inside and outside the house.

9.   Doors, both interior and exterior, are wood panel, often with the upper half glazed.

The glass in exterior doors was an important source of light. A room might have only one window or no window at all, so that the light coming through the door was essential. The popularity of side lights and transoms or glazed door panels during the territorial period explains the origin of this feature of the rural adobes.

Interior doors are also commonly half glass. During the Spanish Colonial period, interior doorways were often hung with cloth. Such doorways still exist in some houses (Figure 98). The glass interior door may be a link between the partial barrier of a cloth and the absolute visual barrier of a solid wood door. In many cases the half-glass interior doors were once exterior doors but were later enclosed by additions.

The configuration of the panels of the doors varies. Most of the doors of the rural adobes in existence today were factory made rather than hand crafted. The factory-made doors often have four vertical panels or five horizontal panels, although many other patterns exist.

10.   The most commonly used door opens directly into the kitchen.

A house often has several doors of apparently equal status, but the most commonly used one gives access to the kitchen, which is typically a warm, spacious room with a table and chairs in the center or occasionally at one end. This room is the heart of the house where family and friends eat and socialize. It has been suggested that a house which opens directly into the main room where the family gathers, without having to pass through an entrance hall, foyer, or intervening rooms, is an indication of a stable, peaceful society where neighbors are trusted.[4]

11.   Interior walls are painted in pastel colors or deeper tints, or covered with wallpaper.

Each room is usually a different color such as pink, yellow, blue, or aqua. Sometimes the paint is applied directly over mud plaster.

Painted or papered wainscots are common, particularly in the kitchen. Kitchens sometimes have a wainscot of heavy plastic-coated paper printed to look like ceramic tile. Paneled walls are becoming more popular, and many rooms now have walls covered with Masonite panels with a dark wood-grain finish.

12.   Ceilings are fiberboard with wood battens.

The fiberboard panels are attached to the underside of the vigas or joists (Figure 97). In some cases the panels are furred down in order to lower the ceiling. Wood lath strips about one-fourth by one and one-fourth inches are used as battens to cover the seams between the fiberboard panels. A few ceilings are made of narrow tongue-and-groove boards with a beaded edge (Figure 102). The ceilings are painted the same color as the walls or a contrasting color or white. Pressed tin ceilings are quite rare. Half a dozen manta ceilings and one corrugated metal ceiling were found as well as a few ceilings with exposed vigas or hewn beams. More recent ceilings are often gypsum board or acoustic tile.

13.   The houses were built as a series of plain rectangular rooms.

The houses were built without halls, closets, or bathrooms in the same manner as the Spanish Colonial houses and early Yankee houses in the territory. Most rural adobes built before the Second World War have bathrooms added later by partitioning an original room or by adding onto the original house. Halls and closets sometimes were built in conjunction with the new bathroom. This interior partitioning was nearly always carried out in wood frame construction rather than adobe or concrete block.

The characteristics listed above are shared by most of the older houses of rural northern New Mexico. Other features occur frequently but less predictably throughout the region. For example, there are several common ways to reach the attic. About half the houses have interior stairways. These stairs are often in the kitchen, which is convenient if the attic is used for drying food. The stairway is narrow, and usually steep. Often it is L-shaped with the upper part enclosed with wood framing so that it is necessary to pass through the doorway on about the fourth or fifth step (Figure 101). Sometimes the stair is open, with a simple wooden balustrade and a trap door at the top (Figure 102). Houses without interior stairs have access to the attic by means of a movable ladder or a permanent exterior stair leading to a gable door (Figure 64).

Roof ladders are a common sight on many of the rural houses throughout the region. They are homemade, using milled lumber. The most usual form has rungs spanning two side rails, but sometimes they are a single board with footholds nailed across it at right angles. The ladder hangs on the pitched roof by one or two boards which hook over the ridge. The ladder can be moved along the ridge as needed for roof maintenance. (See Figure 5.)

The corrugated steel has changed very little in appearance during this century, but the common gauge has become gradually thinner. Corrugated steel available before World War I had a useful life span of seventy or eighty years. Since then, the commonly used material has become thinner, and the lifespan has been reduced to about fifty years or less.

The gables of the rural houses are made of a variety of materials. Most are either wood frame or adobe. The wood framing may be covered with boards, asphalt shingles, wood shingles, or tar paper. The gable sometimes has a diamond-shaped window near the top. Such windows occur here and there throughout the region and seem to have been popular from about 1905 until 1940. (See Figure 26.)

Window styles are varied. Virtually all the windows are manufactured rather than homemade. The six-over-six double-hung wood window was the first type of manufactured window used in the territory (Figure 21). The oldest type most frequently seen in the villages today is the two-over-two double-hung wood window which was widely available from 1880 to about 1910 (Figure 71). The one-over-one double-hung became available in about 1900 and is also fairly common in the rural houses (Figure 70). The four-over-four style was also used around the turn of the century. During the 1930s and 1940s three-over-one and four-over-one windows (three or four tall narrow panes arranged side by side in the upper sash) were quite common (Figure 18). Wood casement windows were used from about 1920 until about 1950. These usually have two sashes side by side, each two panes wide and two, three, or four panes high (Figure 48). The factory-made sashes were set in homemade frames. Steel casement windows and aluminum sliding windows were commonly used after World War II.

The original windows of a house are sometimes replaced with newer windows, and recycled windows are sometimes built into new construction. These practices of replacing and reusing windows combined with the practice of building a house in stages over a period of time have produced many houses that have a variety of window types that do not readily indicate the age of the house.

Portal posts are usually slender. Various houses throughout the region have round factory-made columns turned on a lathe with an ornate spindle and ball pattern. These were used during the Victorian era by owners who could afford them. Most home builders made their own portal posts out of milled lumber with square sections. In the Peñasco area these square columns were often faceted in ways to suggest the factory-made columns.

Owners who could afford the luxury of pure ornament bought or made brackets for the portal columns. The factory-made brackets came by rail to New Mexico. Their complex, ornate forms reflect the popularity of the gingerbread style throughout the nation at the turn of the century. Homemade brackets were simpler by necessity and often quite original. Brackets usually appear in villages where portales were built before World War II by owners who could afford a little style. Brazos and Los Ojos have quite a few houses with brackets on the portal and other examples are scattered throughout the region. (See Figure 53.)

Cellars under the houses are very rare although food storage rooms or despensas are often dug into a hillside to take advantage of the cool stable temperature of the surrounding earth. These are small one-room structures with a single door. (See Figure 55.)

In certain villages a few houses are contiguous and have party walls. These are often remnants of a placita settlement with houses joined together and facing inward for protection from Indians, although the custom is typical throughout Latin America, apart from concerns about frontier dangers. There are joined houses in San José, Llano, Villanueva, Dixon, Mora, and elsewhere, but the best examples are found at the old Plaza del Cerro in Chimayó (Figure 19).

Similar to the joined houses but less common are the divided houses. Occasionally one sees a single free-standing house with a continuous roof line which is half one color and half another, or has a front yard and portal split in two by a picket fence (Figure 96). Through inheritance these houses have come to be owned by separate but usually related families. In some of the old, densely built villages, the distinction between joined houses and divided houses may blur as contiguous structures are divided and combined in different ways over generations.

Figure 52. This store in Vallecitos was added to a pitched-roof adobe, probably in the 1920s. These unusual homemade brackets are repeated on a house in nearby Cañon Plaza and may have inspired the butterfly brackets of a second house in Cañon Plaza.

CUARTELES LOS OJOS TRUCHAS VELARDE

DIXON MORA CAÑON PLAZA LAS VEGAS

Figure 53. Only a few of the rural adobes have brackets at the portal columns. At least half of the brackets in the region are homemade. The

102

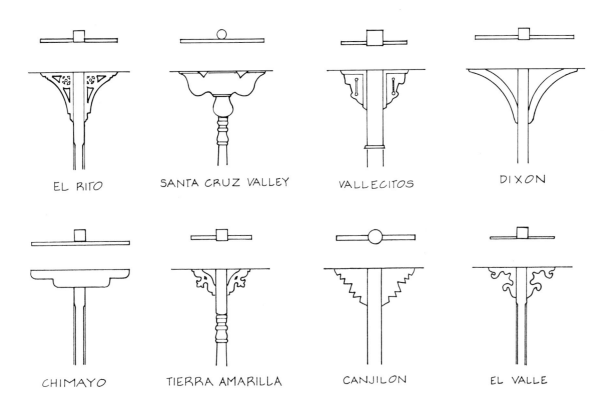

EL RITO   SANTA CRUZ VALLEY   VALLECITOS   DIXON

CHIMAYO   TIERRA AMARILLA   CANJILON   EL VALLE

wide range of patterns and color schemes lend an appealing individuality
to a number of houses.

Figure 54. This little salmon-colored house in Cañon Plaza has a picket fence at the portal, a common feature derived from the nineteenth-century Territorial balustrade. Note the homemade butterfly brackets, which are quite inventive.

Figure 55. Despensas, used for food storage, are often built into the hill-side. This one in Chimayó is larger than many.

Figure 56. A type of construction seen occasionally in northern New Mexico consists of wood framing covered with boards, then diagonal strips of wood lath plastered with mud. The weathered surface has exposed the lath on this little building in Tierra Amarilla.

Figure 57. A doorway in Las Trampas has a homemade door which incorporates a factory-made glazed sash. The white dado and the blue wall have been freshly painted.

Figure 58. The sloped head and splayed jambs of this Cordova doorway and the corner braces of the screen door are more exaggerated than most found in the area. Note the weathered mud plaster.

Figure 59. Classic Territorial doorways like this Las Vegas example with transom and side lights are more apt to be found on the east side of the Sangre de Cristos and along the Pecos River than elsewhere in the region. The classical pilasters of the door frame are rarely seen on simple adobe houses. The door is factory-made Victorian.

Figure 60. The waisted door jambs of this Santa Cruz Valley house are made by adding a little piece of wood at the base. The flaired or winged pediment is also characteristic of the area.

110

Figure 61. This doorway in Petaca has a sloped head in addition to the characteristic splayed jambs. The door itself has the usual half-glass over recessed panels painted a contrasting color.

Figure 62. This type of decorative door is locally made and characteristic of Peñasco, though very few remain.

Figure 63. This homemade door in Llano is white with blue accents. The hasp and padlock are commonly used in this way throughout the region.

Figure 64. This three-room house in El Valle was built in the 1920s. The gable has pressed metal siding imitating ashlar stone which is unusual. The squat gable door is handmade. The house has grey stucco with white and green trim.

Figure 65. This simple house in Llano has a movable ladder giving access to the attic through a window. The house has grey stucco with white and green trim.

Figure 66. This Llano house has two-toned woodwork typical of the area. The woodwork is green and white. The walls are apple green with a dark red painted dado. The roof is beginning to rust, showing the spacing of the boards beneath. The hipped-roof portal is fairly common.

116

Figure 67. This house in Llano was probably built in the nineteenth century, judging from the long linear form, the height of the walls, and the decorative handmade door. The roof and portal are much more recent. The left half is light blue under the portal with white trim. The right half is brown with brown columns.

Figure 68. The simple door flanked by two casement windows of this Truchas house is a common feature throughout the region, particularly in the villages west of the Sangre de Cristo Mountains. It is a local twentieth-century interpretation of the earlier Territorial doorway with side lights.

Figure 69. This east-facing wing of an **L**-shaped Chimayó house has a door flanked by two casement windows. The house has peach-colored stucco and a very rusted roof.

Figure 70. This peach-colored Los Ojos house has white trim. The ceiling of the portal is beaded board siding painted light blue. The ornate columns and brackets, the gable dormers, and the portal wrapped around the gable end are features common in that area.

Figure 71.   The tall, narrow gable dormers on the steeply pitched roof give credence to the report that this house in La Puente predates 1912. The tar-paper roofing is badly deteriorated, having a useful life of about twenty years, compared to about sixty years for corrugated steel.

Figure 72. This house in the Santa Cruz Valley east of La Puebla has pale salmon walls, white under the portal, and mint green trim. It was bought in 1943 in its present condition. The house has an interior enclosed stair.

Figure 73. The decorative elements at the top of the columns are an unusual shape. The winged pediments over windows and doors are common in the Santa Cruz Valley. The board floor of the portal is typical, though many have now been replaced with concrete.

Figure 74. The Chavez house in El Duende just above the conflux of the Ojo Caliente and the Chama rivers had a flat roof until the early 1950s, when the present roof was built. The portal was added shortly thereafter. The house has aqua walls with white trim.

Local Themes

The isolation of the individual villages and the strong family ties within each village have resulted in local themes within the rural adobe style. In 1935 in the area north of Santa Fe between the Sangre de Cristos and the Jemez Mountains, less than one family in six had a car or a truck. Roads were poor. The Tewa Basin Study noted the difference in behavioral style of the people from one village to the next as well as the difference in physical appearance of the communities. Traditionally, houses were built by the owner with help from family and friends within the community. This mutual cooperation probably contributed to the proliferation of a motif or detail within an area, although imitation of an admired prototype is probably the key factor.

A few of these local variations are quite obvious and remarkable, like the tricolor woodwork and diamond columns, but others, such as the transom, are not readily noticeable. Some of these variations are predominant in one village only; others are charcteristic for a whole area within the region. None is so consistent as to be predictably found in one village or area or to be completely absent elsewhere.

Among the noticeable regional variations in style are the following:

1.   The small central porch is common in the Mora area, including Cleveland and Holman. The little porch protects the door which is centered in a symmetrical façade. The porch has two wood columns and a frontal gable, hipped, or shed roof. In many cases there is a balustrade, and sometimes there are benches placed at each side of the porch facing one another. (See Figure 40.)

2.   The transom is most common on the east side of the Sangre de Cristos, which had more early Anglo influence than the west side, with the exception of Santa Fe and perhaps Taos. The transom is seen more often in Sapello, Cleveland, Mora, Ledoux, Upper Rociada, Las Vegas, San Miguel, and Villanueva than in most of the villages in the Río Grande Valley to the west. The transom was a common nineteenth-century detail of American architecture. Its appearance on certain houses of the eastern slopes and the Pecos Valley is an indicator of the age of those houses and the relative prosperity of the owners at that time. The transom remained popular during the very early part of the twentieth century. (See Figure 59.)

3.   The gabled wall dormer is a common feature in Wagon Mound and in the Tierra Amarilla area, with other scattered examples within the Chama River basin. It is one of the oldest of the dormered pitched-roof styles. The house walls generally continue above the second-floor framing, creating a spacious attic or second story. (See Figures 92 and 108.)

4.   Diamond columns are a common motif in Peñasco, Rodarte, Llano, and El Valle. They are made locally from square columns and usually have two or three bands of diamond facets. The recessed facets are usually painted one color, the diamonds another, and sometimes the basic column is a third color. The rest of the woodwork of the house is usually simple and painted in the same two or three colors. The diamond columns probably date to the 1940s or possibly earlier. They appear to be a local interpretation of the ornate, factory-made, turned Victorian columns which were occasionally used in the more prosperous villages throughout the region. (See Figures 80 and 81.)

5.   The patterned shingle gable is a popular detail in Truchas and nearby Córdova and Las Trampas (Figure 87). The motif is part of the Queen Anne style and was originally made with wood shingles of different shapes to form banded patterns. One example of these wood shingles can still be seen in Truchas, but more recently the motif has been carried out with rolls of asphalt shingles with exposed hexagonal edges. Various patterns were achieved by alternating rows of different colors, normally red and green. One very old and abandoned house in Ojo Sarco had an entire pitched roof of the red and green patterned shingles. Lucía Vigil, whose house in Trampas was built in 1947, replaced the red and green hexagonal shingles of the gable last year because they were worn out. She tried to find new red and green hexagonal shingles but could not, so she settled for straight-cut shingles which, when alternated, created red and green horizontal stripes.

6.   The gable balcony and stair is common in Tierra Amarilla, Los Ojos, and Los Brazos, and can be seen elsewhere in the Chama Valley. There is an old gable-front store in Tierra Amarilla with the date 1884 on the façade. The gable projects over a second-story balcony above the entrance portal. This building might have served as a prototype for houses with a second-story balcony under a projected eave. A covered access to the attic was important during the long, snowy winters in the Tierra Amarilla area. (See Figure 78.)

7.   The ridge dormer is a dormer whose roof is the continuation of the main roof of the house. The dormer has vertical sides and the dormer roof is hipped. These are not very common, but their occurrence seems to be most frequent in Chimayó and the nearby Santa Cruz Valley. This style seems to have been most popular in the 1940s. (See Figure 82.)

8.   The cross gable has a triangular face and a pitched roof formed by two triangular roof sections. It is the most common form of dormer in Ojo Caliente and is also popular at La Madera about ten miles to the north. (See Figure 83.)

9.   The sloped door frame heads exist primarily in Truchas, Las Trampas, Llano, and Córdova. The splayed window and door jambs were a common feature in the nineteenth-century house styles imported from the United States. The window and door jambs of rural adobe houses are often splayed. The sloped head seems to be an elaboration on this theme. It occurs in areas which have almost no transoms, so the sloped head may have been used to add height to the door frame and to compensate visually for the lack of a transom. (See Figure 58.)

10.   Double interior French doors were found in some of the Truchas houses and in one Mora house but are fairly uncommon. They were added in a Las Vegas house as part of a 1932 remodeling. Single interior glass doors are common throughout the region.

11.   The open stair and trap door are common in the Chimayó and Truchas area. The stair is most often in the kitchen and has a simple painted wood balustrade. It is sometimes straight and sometimes L-shaped but is always against a wall and gives access to a trap door in the floor of the attic. (See Figure 102.)

12.   Waisted door and window casings occur on a few houses, primarily in the Santa Cruz Valley. This casing profile is a Victorian feature belonging to the Italianate style popular in the United States from 1840 to 1885. As a local theme in rural northern New Mexico, it was popular around the 1920s. (See Figure 60.)

13.   Winged pediments are common in the Santa Cruz Valley.

The ends of the window and door pediments curve outward beyond the edge of the jambs. This profile suggests the more complicated Greek Revival pediment built up from a number of wood moldings. (See Figure 60.)

14. **White scalloped brackets** are common in Truchas. They approximate the profile of corbels but are cut from thin boards and nailed to the front face of the portal columns.

These local themes are a part of the traditional adobe style of the northern New Mexico villages. Houses in the rural areas continue to be owner-built so that more recent local themes are also evident. The following local themes are more recent and diverge too radically from the general character of the older rural adobes to be considered a part of the traditional rural style, yet they are an outgrowth of it, and they demonstrate continued vitality in creating and perpetuating local themes.

Among the more recent local themes one finds the following:

1. **The repeated frontal gable** of Mora and Cleveland appears to be a fairly recent development. The house has a gabled front façade, with a smaller gabled façade of similar proportions projected from the main façade. The repeated frontal gable was a popular feature during the early twentieth century throughout the United States. This composition is similar to the simple frontal gable which is a common element in Mora dating from the early territorial period.

2. **Rope columns** are heavy square wood columns incised with parallel diagonal lines running around all four sides of the column. Sometimes the column is set at 45° to the porch so the corner of the column is dominant and shows a series of V-shaped incisions. These columns are used on small, often inset porches of compact houses. The columns are stained and varnished more often than painted. Their popularity ranges from the Santa Cruz Valley along Highway 76 to Peñasco, and they are also quite popular in Taos.

3.   Exterior masonry wainscots have become commonplace in the Santa Cruz Valley, Truchas, and Peñasco. They are usually brick, though stone and slump block are sometimes used. This recent theme may be a continuation of the combined elements of the painted dado and the concrete protection veneer, but it has a modern look quite different from the earlier treatments. It appears on suburban-style houses rather than traditional adobes.

4.   Hip-on-gable roofs are a recent development in Peñasco, often appearing on compact houses with low pitched roofs. The ridge of the pitched roof ends in a small hip roof so the top of the gable is truncated.

Figure 75. The little hipped roof beneath the gable of this Truchas house occurs occasionally throughout the region, giving added protection to walls that were once mud plastered. The thin corbel-shaped brackets show the influence of the Santa Fe style. The interior has several French doors. The door frames have splayed jambs and sloped heads.

Figure 76. This Las Vegas house has an open exterior stair to the attic. The plywood diamond pattern on the picket fence was also seen on an interior stair balustrade in Mora.

Figure 77. The Rafael Martínez house in Los Ojos has an interior stair leading to rooms above. The house was built with the hip roof during the early 1900s. The two-tone turned columns and factory-made ornate brackets are typical in Los Ojos.

Figure 78. Two contiguous houses form this large structure in Brazos. The original wood shingles were replaced with corrugated steel in about 1925. The projected gable roof covering the stair is typical in the area.

Figure 79. This diminutive house in Cleveland is a curious example of the compact symmetrical cottage with frontal gable porch over the center doorway. The original wood windows were three-over-one pattern and have been replaced very recently with smaller aluminum windows. The walls are green stucco, the woodwork is white, and the corrugated metal roof has been painted brown.

Figure 80. The Romero House in El Valle has pink walls with green gables and white columns with red diamonds on deep blue. Corn and chiles are drying on the portal.

Figure 81. The north portal of the Gonzáles house in Llano has mint green walls and white columns with white diamonds on a red background. The rafter ends are also painted red. The wire strung along the portal posts is used for drying clothes and is a common feature. The pitched roof was added to the house in 1947.

Figure 82. This compact house in the Santa Cruz Valley was built in 1943. The porch appears to be a more recent addition. There is no interior stair. The ridge dormers are popular in the area.

Figure 83. Cross gables are characteristic of the Ojo Caliente region. This house is 121 years old, but the roof and portal are more recent. The screened-in portal is rare, although a few portals throughout the region have been recently glazed with rigid plastic for solar heat.

Figure 84. This house on Prince Avenue in Española was built in 1935. It has six rooms of approximately equal size. An **L**-shaped enclosed stair leads from the kitchen to the attic. The roof has been painted light red.

Figure 85.   The Serna house in Hernández, when bought in 1937, was a flat-roofed two-room adobe. In 1950, the kitchen, bath, and several other rooms were added and the pitched roof was built. The roof design was copied from the Prince Avenue house which is a mile or two to the south. The house is light green with white trim. There is an interior trap door to the attic but no stair.

Figure 86. U-shaped houses are far less common than L-shaped houses. This one in Brazos has wall dormers and a dropped portal characteristic of the area.

Figure 87. This garage in Peñasco has a patterned shingle gable. Horizontal rows of hexagonally cut red and green asphalt shingles are alternated and offset, resulting in vertical bands of red and green. Patterned shingle gables are common in Peñasco and Truchas.

Inside and Out

The interiors of inhabited houses are furnished in a modest and comfortable way. They are generally altered and renewed periodically and cannot be dated to a past era as the exteriors often are. The kitchens sometimes have remarkably old wood-burning stoves. Curtains, upholstery, carpets, and needlework of various sorts give the houses a warm, comfortable feeling. Usually a number of family photographs are hung on the walls or displayed on a tabletop. White lace curtains cover the windows and the glass of the doors.

The interiors of the houses bear little resemblance to the interiors of colonial adobes. The sparseness is gone. There are no more corner fireplaces. In some cases, ceilings have been lowered to make them more accessible for cleaning, and perhaps to make the room easier to heat. The floors are usually covered with linoleum or wall-to-wall carpet. The most distinguishing features that remain are the thick adobe walls. The woodwork of old doorways and windows penetrating the thick walls gives a unique character to the interiors of many rural houses.

Most of the houses have no dining room because the kitchen is large and has a table and chairs. The living room may be no larger than the kitchen and does not often feel like the most important room of the house.

The exterior realm of the rural adobe does retain a strong link to its colonial heritage in that the surrounding space is of little importance both practically and esthetically. Traditionally the adobe houses turned inward, with outdoor activities taking place in the courtyard or patio. The space outside these houses was not part of the realm of the house, so was left undeveloped and unattended except as farming needs dictated. Today the rural houses have no enclosed patios adjoining the houses. In many cases, the portal has become the only exterior space directly related to the house. Often the portal is enclosed with a picket fence and a small gate usually at one end. This may serve a practical purpose in keeping dogs and small children in or out, but it also defines the space as private. The portal area is used for various purposes including sitting, wood storage, clotheslines, and food drying. In such cases where the portal is the only apparent outdoor living space, the remaining area around the house has a random character. Acequias, outbuildings, trees, and bare dirt areas used for parking all occur, but in no obvious relationship to the house.

In other cases a maintained yard exists. It is a relatively small area often enclosed by a picket or a wire fence, or a low wall. High solid walls are noticeably absent. It has a walkway of some sort to the portal and some sort of planting, either grass or trees or flowerbeds. Planting is kept away from the base of the walls to reduce moisture problems and avoid damage from roots. A maintained area is as likely to be compacted earth cleared of weeds and swept, as to be planted with vegetation.

The placement and orientation of the houses appear to be somewhat random because a variety of factors influence the siting of a house.

In the earliest instances houses were joined together to form a defensive plaza; later, individual houses were located at convenient spots near the center of the village or close to the owner's irrigated land. As new generations grew up and married, houses were added to the family lands at whatever spot seemed the most available and suitable. The site needed to be well drained, level, and accessible from the road. The houses are usually placed parallel or perpendicular to the road, though they may not face it. A few are obliquely placed. The more recent houses with compact floor plans usually face the road squarely.

These rural houses continue to evolve and to reflect the needs and the preferences of their owners. In contrast to the few traditional materials of the older houses, the newer houses incorporate a wider variety of materials. For example, the recent trend has been to use filigree iron portal posts instead of wood columns. The appearance of the newer houses is suburban. Most of the newer houses are built in areas where local business or government activity provides an economic base for the community, such as Española, the Santa Cruz Valley, and Peñasco. Other communities such as Ojo Sarco and Dixon have new houses, built by counter-culture Anglos, which have a style all their own. The smaller and more remote villages have very little new construction, although houses are torn down or remodeled from time to time. While the traditional rural adobes have given way to more recent styles, and those that remain are threatened with decay and drastic remodeling, an interest in them is emerging in Santa Fe. A few examples of new pitched metal roof houses which take their exterior form from the rural adobes have been built in Santa Fe and nearby communities.

These new urban copies are, of course, different from the rural adobes just as any revival style shares only superficial aspects with the original one. The circumstances and influences that produced the rural adobes have nearly disappeared. The remaining houses of the rural adobe style represent a unique architectural expression which emerged, flourished, and died out over a period of about one hundred years.

The special value of these houses stems from their unique cultural roots. If Latin America is that part of the Western Hemisphere where Spaniards conquered, colonized, and founded an enduring and dominant Hispanic culture, then northern New Mexico is the northernmost reach of Latin America. The reason why New Mexico was so slow to be granted statehood (1912 for New Mexico as compared, for example, to 1864 for Nevada, 1876 for Colorado, and 1890 for Wyoming) is that New Mexico was essentially a foreign land inhabited by a non–English-speaking population which had a stable culture distinctly different from the Anglo culture of the United States.

Because the Hispanic culture of New Mexico has endured and has remained dominant in large areas of northern New Mexico, the architecture of the region has continued to be distinct, original, and dynamic. Architectural fashions popular elsewhere in the United States were certainly adopted but were also transformed to suit local ways and means. The evolution of rural New Mexico houses accepted outside ideas, motifs, and technology, but generally the houses were built in accordance with regional or even local (i.e., the village) building traditions. Very few old houses in the rural areas of the region are typical of American houses of the period. The widespread and consistent use of adobe, the tradition of the owner-built house, and the relative isolation of the villages all contributed to the perpetuation and vitality of the rural style. The stability and longevity of the traditional building methods surviving from the Spanish Colonial period provided a solid framework in which to incorporate architectural influences from outside the region.

The result is a collection of rural houses, decaying but still handsome, still inhabited for the most part by the people who built them, and still sited within their original context. The acequias are still flowing, hay is still cut seasonally for a few horses in the fields here and there, and the sons and daughters come home from the city on the weekends. The villages, although struggling to stay alive, are still bearing witness to a past era of economic independence and social vitality which produced these extraordinary houses.

Figure 88. The Epifanio Martínez house in the Santa Cruz Valley is no longer inhabited. It was built by the grandparents of Epifanio Martínez in the late 1800s. The kitchen, shown on the left, was built first. The middle room was added later and finally the end room at the right. The pitched roof and the stair in the kitchen were added before 1925. Each of the three rooms has one window and one exterior door. The exterior walls are mud plastered.

Figure 89. An interior communicating door of the Epifanio Martínez house showing the splayed wood door frame set in the thick adobe wall.

Figure 90. The room on the south end of the Epifanio Martínez house has a steep open stair to the attic which was built when the pitched roof was added to the house. The house is being used for hay storage.

Figure 91. The attic of the Epifanio Martínez house has a dirt floor. The chimneys pass through the space at the left. The skin of a deer or an elk has been laid on the floor to dry.

Figure 92. The Eluterio Martínez house in Tierra Amarilla had a single story until it was remodeled and enlarged in the 1930s. A stairway in the central hall leads to the five upstairs rooms.

Figure 93. An upstairs window of the Eluterio Martínez house shows the thickness of the adobe compared to the wood framing of the gable wall. The Victorian columns and brackets of the upstairs balcony can be seen beyond.

Figure 94. The Olivario Romero house in El Valle was built in 1925 and is now being used for storage. The portal columns are white with green accents. The mud-plastered exterior is painted yellow under the portal. There are three rooms downstairs and three upstairs.

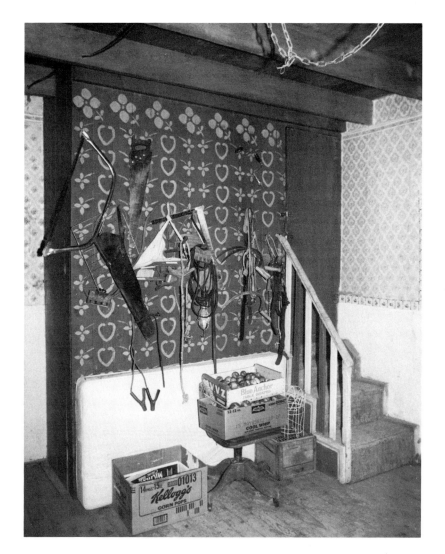

Figure 95. The stair of the Olivario Romero house in El Valle is a typical **L**-shaped enclosed stair. The boards that enclosed the stair are dark green with hand-painted yellow designs. The railing has alternating yellow and green balusters.

Figure 96. The north half (on the right) of this structure in Tierra Amarilla is owned by Esperidion and Antonia Martínez. The south wing of the structure is the oldest part. The last two rooms were added and the entire structure was given a pitched roof in about 1911. The stair in the north half has been relocated twice.

Figure 97. The living room of the Esperidion Martínez house has a panel and batten ceiling which is characteristic of rural adobe houses.

Figure 98. The bedroom of the Esperidion Martínez house has exposed vigas which is uncommon. The ceiling is painted a pastel color. The doorway to the right is draped with cloth and leads to an adjoining room.

Figure 99. The north wing of the attic of the Esperidion Martínez house is used for drying chile in the fall.

Figure 100. The east wing of the attic of the Esperidion Martínez house contains two bedrooms. Such upstairs rooms are fairly uncommon except in the Tierra Amarilla area.

Figure 101. The Martínez house in Brazos (Figure 45) has two interior **L**-shaped enclosed stairs. This one probably appears much as it did when it was built around the turn of the century.

Figure 102. The open stair of the Ortega house in Chimayó leads from the kitchen through a trap door to the attic. The wood ceiling of this room was added in the 1930s replacing a manta ceiling.

Figure 103. The kitchen of the Felipe Valdez house (Figure 28) in Brazos has a linoleum floor, a board ceiling, and a coated paper wainscot.

Figure 104. The woodburning stove of the Felipe Valdez house keeps the kitchen warm throughout the year.

Figure 105. This particular room of the Trujillo house (Figure 46) in Córdova has a manta ceiling of brown figured cloth. Such ceilings, reminiscent of the Colonial era, are rare today. The higher floor level of the adjoining room is an indication that the adjoining room may be older than this room.

Figure 106. The left half of this Chimayó house was built by a young couple in 1905. The right half was built by their daughter and son-in-law in 1933. The pitched metal roof was built over the entire structure in 1938. The concrete protection veneer was added in 1970.

Figure 107. This authentic old portal in Vallecitos has a board floor and a beaded board ceiling. It was built in the 1910s or 1920s. The baseboard at the juncture of the porch floor and the house wall is a common feature of early portales. The house, with its triangular pediments over the doors and windows, may be several decades older.

Figure 108. The Gárcia house in Wagon Mound is typical of a particular type of house there. These houses have a living room downstairs and a kitchen usually with a narrow **L**-shaped open stair and a simple wood balustrade. There are one or more bedrooms upstairs lit by wall dormers. The houses are one room deep and generally only two rooms wide. This particular house has green stucco with white trim.

Figure 109. The Montoya house is another example of the two-story dormered houses popular in Wagon Mound in the early 1900s. Most of these houses have a lean-to addition attached to the back of the original house. Unlike the two-story houses of Tierra Amarilla and elsewhere in the Chama River valley, these houses have a diminutive scale and lack the long continuous portales. The lawn and concrete curb and gutter are incongruous with most of the New Mexico villages, but Wagon Mound was developed as a railroad town with a typical grid of wide, straight streets.

Notes

Chapter 1: Today

1. Marc Simmons, "Settlement Patterns and Village Plans in Colonial New Mexico," 104.

Chapter 2: Early Spanish Settlements

1. Myra Ellen Jenkins, "Some Eighteenth Century New Mexico Women of Property," 340.
2. Bainbridge Bunting, "Architecture of the Embudo Watershed," 19.

Chapter 3: The Hispanic Legacy

1. Among the best sources are E. Boyd, Roland F. Dickey, and Sytha Motto.
2. Marian Russell, *Land of Enchantment: Memoirs of Marian Russell along the Santa Fe Trail*, 38.
3. James F. Meline, *Two Thousand Miles on Horseback*, 151.
4. Roland F. Dickey, *New Mexico Village Arts*, 42.
5. Sytha Motto, *Old Houses of New Mexico and the People Who Built Them*, 3.
6. Josiah Gregg, *Commerce of the Prairies*, 145.
7. Sytha Motto, *Old Houses of New Mexico and the People Who Built Them*, 14; and W. W. H. Davis, *El Gringo, New Mexico and Her People*, 177.

Chapter 4:   Yankee Newcomers

1. *The Daily Picayune*, New Orleans, April 17, 1840.
2. Josiah Gregg, *Commerce of the Prairies*, 106.
3. W. W. H. Allison, "Santa Fe in 1846," 401.
4. Mary J. Straw, *Loretto; The Sisters and Their Santa Fe Chapel*, 34.
5. Colonel George Archibald McCall, *New Mexico in 1850: A Military View*, 47.
6. Most Reverend John Baptiste Salpointe, D. D., *Soldiers of the Cross*, 235.
7. Frances Leon Swadesh, *Los Primeros Pobladores*, 143.

Chapter 5:   Birth of a Style

1. Fray Angélico Chávez, *My Penitente Land*, 251.
2. Josiah Gregg, *Commerce of the Prairies*, 145–46.
3. Christopher Wilson, *Architecture and Preservation in Las Vegas, Vol. II: New Districts, New Developments*, 31.
4. Roland F. Dickey, *New Mexico Village Arts*, 62.
5. Sytha Motto, *Old Houses of New Mexico and the People Who Built Them*, 15.

Chapter 6:   Evolution

1. The Tewa Basin Study is a 1935 report by the United States Department of the Interior which addressed the population, health, schools, economic conditions, and distinguishing features of communities in north-central New Mexico. Volume II of the study has been reprinted with supplementary materials under the title *Hispanic Villages of Northern New Mexico*, edited by Marta Weigle and published by the Lightning Tree Press.
2. Melicendro Martínez, personal interview, October 13, 1983.
3. James F. Meline, *Two Thousand Miles on Horseback*, 105.
4. Virginia Ortega, personal interview, November 11, 1983.

Chapter 7:   Fundamentals of the Rural Adobe

1. Roland F. Dickey, *New Mexico Village Arts*, 45.
2. James A. Michner, *Iberia*, 173.
3. Roland F. Dickey, *New Mexico Village Arts*, 62.
4. Henry Glassie, *Folk Housing in Middle Virginia*, 190.

Bibliography

Adams, Robert. *The Architecture and Art of Early Hispanic Colorado*. Boulder: Colorado Associated University Press, 1974.

Allison, W. W. H. "Santa Fe in 1846", *Old Santa Fe* 2, 4 (April 1915): 392–406.

Bell, William A. *New Tracks in North America*. Albuquerque: Horn and Wallace, Publishers, 1965.

Beck, Warren A., and Ynez D. Haase. *Historical Atlas of New Mexico*. Norman: University of Oklahoma Press, 1969.

Borhegyi, Stephan F. de. "The Evolution of a Landscape," *Landscape* 4 (Summer 1954): 24–30.

Boyd, E. *Popular Arts of Spanish New Mexico*. Santa Fe: Museum of New Mexico Press, 1974.

Brown, Lorin W. *Hispano Folklife of New Mexico*. Albuquerque: University of New Mexico Press, 1978.

Bullock, Alice. *Mountain Villages* Santa Fe: Sunstone Press, 1973.

Bunting, Bainbridge. *Early Architecture in New Mexico*. Albuquerque: University of New Mexico Press, 1976.

———*Of Earth and Timbers Made*. Albuquerque: University of New Mexico Press, 1974.

———"Take a Trip with NMA, An Architectural Guide to Northern New Mexico," *New Mexico Architecture*: 12, 9 and 10 (Sept.–Oct. 1970): 13–47.

————*Taos Adobes*. Santa Fe: Museum of New Mexico Press, 1964.

————"The Penitente Upper Morada," *New Mexico Architecture*: 4, 9 and 10 (Sept.–Oct. 1962): 15–17.

————"Architecture of the Embudo Watershed," *New Mexico Architecture* (May–June 1962): 19–26.

Byne, Arthur, and Mildred Stapley. *Spanish Interiors and Furniture*. New York: Dover Publications, 1969.

Carver, Norman F., Jr. *Iberian Villages*. Kalamazoo: Documan Press, Ltd., 1981.

Chávez, Fray Angélico. *My Penitente Land*. Albuquerque: University of New Mexico Press, 1974.

Conway, A. W. "A Northern New Mexico House Type," *Landscape* 1, (Autumn 1951): 20–1.

Davis, W. W. H. *El Gringo, New Mexico and Her People*. Lincoln: University of Nebraska Press, 1982.

Dickey, Roland F. *New Mexico Village Arts*. Albuquerque: University of New Mexico Press, 1949.

Emmett, Chris. *Fort Union and the Winning of the Southwest*. Norman: University of Oklahoma Press, 1965.

Emory, Lieutenant W. H. *Lieutenant Emory Reports: Notes of a Military Reconnaissance*. Albuquerque: University of New Mexico Press, 1951.

Glassie, Henry. *Folk Housing in Middle Virginia*. Knoxville: University of Tennessee Press, 1975.

Gregg, Josiah. *Commerce of the Prairies*. Norman: University of Oklahoma Press, 1954.

Gritzner, Charles F. "Log Housing in New Mexico," *Pioneer America* 3, 2 (July 1971): 54–62.

Hanosh, Eugene J. "A *History of Mora*." Master's thesis, New Mexico Highlands University, 1967.

Holmes, Viviana Nigro. "*Architectural Woodwork of Colonial and Territorial New Mexico*." Ph.D. dissertation, University of New Mexico, 1979.

Horgan, Paul. *Great River: The Río Grande in North American History.* New York: Rinehart & Company, 1954.

Jackson, J. B. "First Comes the House," *Landscape* 9, 2 (Winter 1959 to 60): 26–32.

James, General Thomas. *Three Years Among the Indians and Mexicans.* New York: The Citadel Press, 1966.

Jenkins, Myra Ellen. "Some Eighteenth Century New Mexico Women of Property," in *Hispanic Arts and Ethnohistory in the Southwest,* edited by Marta Weigle, Santa Fe: Ancient City Press, 1983.

Kutsche, Paul, and John R. Van Ness. *Cañones.* Albuquerque: University of New Mexico Press, 1981.

LaFarge, Oliver. *Santa Fe.* Norman: University of Oklahoma Press, 1959.

Larson, Robert W. *New Mexico's Quest for Statehood.* Albuquerque: University of New Mexico Press, 1968.

Lufkin, Agnesa Burney. *"Domestic Architecture in Northeastern New Mexico, Late Territorial Period: 1880–1912."* Ph.D. dissertation, University of New Mexico, 1985.

McAlester, Virginia and Lee. *A Field Guide to American Houses.* New York: Alfred A. Knopf, 1984.

McCall, Colonel George Archibald. *New Mexico in 1850: A Military View.* Norman: University of Oklahoma Press, 1968.

McWilliams, Carey. *North from Mexico.* New York: Greenwood Press, 1968.

Magoffin, Susan Shelby. *Down the Santa Fe Trail and into Mexico: The Diary of Susan Shelby Magoffin 1846–1847.* New Haven: Yale University Press, 1926, 1962.

Meline, James F. *Two Thousand Miles on Horseback.* Albuquerque: Horn and Wallace, Publishers, 1966.

Michener, James A. *Iberia.* New York: Random House, 1960.

Motto, Sytha. *Old Houses of New Mexico and the People Who Built Them.* Albuquerque: Calvin Horn Publisher, 1972.

Newcomb, Rexford. *The Old Mission Churches and Historic Houses of California.* Philadelphia: J. B. Lippincott Co., 1925.

New Mexico State Historic Preservation Bureau. *New Mexico Historic Building Inventory Manual.* Revised edition, 1981.

Pike, Zebulon Montgomery. *The Journals of Zebulon Montgomery Pike.* Norman: University of Oklahoma Press, 1966.

Russell, Marian. *Land of Enchantment: Memoirs of Marian Russell Along the Santa Fe Trail.* Albuquerque: University of New Mexico Press, 1981.

Salpointe, Most Reverend John Baptist, D.D. *Soldiers of the Cross.* Albuquerque: Calvin Horn, Publisher, 1967.

Sexton, R. W. *Spanish Influence on American Architecture and Decoration.* New York: Brentano's, 1927.

Simmons, Marc. "Settlement Patterns and Village Plans in Colonial New Mexico," *New Spain's Far Northern Frontier,* edited by David J. Weber. Albuquerque: University of New Mexico Press, 1979.

Smith, G. E. Kidder. *A Pictorial History of Architecture in America.* New York: American Heritage Publishing Co., 1976.

Soule, Winsor. *Spanish Farm Houses and Minor Public Buildings.* New York: Architectural Book Publishing Co., 1924.

Straw, Mary J. *Loretto, The Sisters and Their Santa Fe Chapel.* Santa Fe: West American Publishing, 1983.

Swadesh, Frances Leon. *Los Primeros Pobladores.* Notre Dame: University of Notre Dame Press, 1974.

Weber, David J. *The Taos Trappers.* Norman: University of Oklahoma Press, 1971.

Weigle, Marta. *Hispanic Villages of Northern New Mexico, a Reprint of Volume II of the 1935 Tewa Basin Study, with Supplementary Materials.* Santa Fe: Lightning Tree, 1975.

Whitmore, Jane. *"The Traditional Village of Agua Fria."* Unpublished report submitted to the Historic Preservation Division by Landmarks Preservation Consultants, Santa Fe, 1983.

Wilson, Christopher. *"Architecture and Preservation in Las Vegas, Vol. II: New Districts, New Developments,* for the Citizens' Committee for Historic Preservation, 1982.

———"When the Room is the Hall," Mass 2 (Summer 1984): 17–23.

Index